# ROSIE

Growing up in post-war London, Rosie and her sister Jo spend their days longing for their grandparents' farm, buried deep in the Hampshire countryside — a green paradise of feasts and freedom where they can roam and dream. But when Rosie is ten years old, everything changes. She and Jo lose their father, their London house, their school, their friends, and — most agonisingly of all — their beloved Nanny, Vera, the only adult to have shown them real love and affection. Briskly dispatched to a freezing boarding school in Hertfordshire, they once again feel like imprisoned castaways. But slowly the teenage Rosie escaped from the cold world of the 1950s, into a place of inspiration and mischief, of loving friendships and dedicated teachers, where a young writer is suddenly ready to be born.

*Books by Rose Tremain*
*Published by Ulverscroft:*

THE COLOUR
THE ROAD HOME
TRESPASS
THE GUSTAV SONATA

ROSE TREMAIN

◆

# ROSIE
## Scenes from a Vanished Life

*Complete and Unabridged*

# CHARNWOOD
*Leicester*

First published in Great Britain in 2018 by
Chatto & Windus
London


First Charnwood Edition
published 2019
by arrangement with
Chatto & Windus
Penguin Random House
London

823·914

A catalogue record for this book is available
from the British Library.

ISBN 978–1–4448–4126–8


Published by
F. A. Thorpe (Publishing)
Anstey, Leicestershire

Set by Words & Graphics Ltd.
Anstey, Leicestershire
Printed and bound in Great Britain by
T. J. International Ltd., Padstow, Cornwall

This book is printed on acid-free paper

To the memory of Vera Sturt ('Nan')
and to my beloved grandchildren,
Archie and Martha Rose

# Contents

Paradise............................................1

Cast Away.........................................27

Mother ...........................................42

Angel ............................................64

The English Room.................................85

Teen Music.......................................112

Milton's Oppositions ............................132

'Tits to the Valley' ............................151

Afterword........................................172


List of Illustrations ...........................175

# Paradise

I can remember this: lying in my pram and looking up at a white sky. Across the sky, some lines are drawn, like musical staves. Fluttering shapes arrive and land on the staves: birds on telegraph wires.

My mother used to say, 'You couldn't possibly remember that. Babies can't capture anything, because they have no words. Your mind would have been as empty as the sky you think you saw.'

I would remind her that the sky wasn't empty. It was filled with the descending notes of birds. They settled on the wires. And she would say, 'Don't be silly. You invented that stuff. The first real memory you could possibly have — when you were, say, three or four — would have been of Linkenholt.'

All right, then. Linkenholt. It's clear and present in my mind. The big house stood on a hill in Hampshire, where the wind was always strong. It was never a beauty. The colour of its brick was too screechy a coral red. Its white-painted gables were too massive. It reminded people of a lumpy three-masted ship, riding its waves of green and beautiful land. But all through my childhood, I longed for it — for the moment of walking through its heavy front door and breathing its familiar perfume. What was that perfume? A composite of beeswax furniture polish, Brasso, French cigarettes and dogs. It was the smell of home.

* * *

It wasn't my home.

Linkenholt Manor belonged to my grandparents, Roland and Mabel Dudley. My older sister Jo and I only went there three times a year — Christmas holidays, Easter and summer. But our love for it was uncontainable. Our day-to-day lives in a dark, post-war London were smog-bound, constrained and confined by the walks to school and back, to the Italian corner shop, to the sooty parks, the skating rink, the swimming baths. But at Linkenholt, we were free. Around the house on the hill were spread two thousand acres of chalky farmland, owned by our grandfather, across which, on our Raleigh bicycles, in corduroy dungarees or sometimes improbably dressed as Indian chiefs, we were allowed to roam. These fields and woods, in the 1950s, were some of the loveliest in England. It is not an exaggeration to say that we often felt our London existence to be a kind of exile, from which we longed to escape, a dark dream from which only at Linkenholt would we awake.

And here we came at last: pulling up Linkenholt Hill in a low gear of our mother's Morris Traveller, cruising slowly through Linkenholt village, past the dairy, past the tiny cricket pavilion, past the church where I was christened, then into the gravelled drive, on the border of which three vast elm trees stood like restless giants.

And now, the arrival. Jill, the overfed Springer spaniel, barking. The door opening. The slow emergence of Granny and Grandpop into the porch. Brief contact with the tobacco-tainted scent of their clothes, with the skin of their faces — taut and shiny over Grandpop's skull; soft and powdery, falling in pastry folds, on Granny's cheek — and then the rush past them to where we longed to be: inside the house, feeling it take us in, then hearing the lovely percussion of our feet clicking against the brass rods of the wide stairs.

The room Jo and I shared was at the back, overlooking a rose garden and a wild spinney beyond, where the wind sighed in the night. To drift to sleep to the sound of this wind, knowing that we were 'home', that the morning would lay before us the paradise we kept dreaming of, was to feel drugged with happiness.

★   ★   ★

Linkenholt loved us. That's how it seemed to me, when I was 'Rosie', a very young, ignorant girl. The place gave us its soul and its grandeur, but Granny and Grandpop were heartbroken people who had almost nothing left to give us. They had lost their elder son, also called Roland, aged sixteen, from a burst appendix. He was away at Harrow School when this happened, so they didn't even see him die. Of their remaining two children — our mother, Jane, and our uncle Michael — they loved only Michael. But in the last month of the war, November 1945, Michael Dudley was killed at Fürstenau in Germany. He was twenty-eight. Roland and Mabel went on living, but they never recovered.

They were left with the one child, the middle

child, the girl child, Jane, who seemed to give them no joy at all. Their precious boys were dead. Such scratchings of affection as they had left, they gave to Michael's two sons, Jonathan and Robert, our cousins. Perhaps, when they let Jo and me cycle off down the drive in our Indian feathers, they secretly hoped a few cowboys had strayed out of Wyoming, USA, to Hampshire, England, and would put an end to us — an end to trying to love children who meant almost nothing to them.

The strange thing is, this didn't seem to matter to us. We were never — in my memory, anyway — craven to the grandparents, longing to please them or hoping to be hugged or petted by them. We loved Linkenholt, not them. They were rich and they had created a beautiful world around themselves, and that world was all to us.

A small regiment of servants kept this world shined up. It was human endeavour that gave to the great hallway its perfumed magnificence, that pruned the lavender paths and the fruit trees and the laurel walks of the vast garden. In the kitchen, huge roasts and puddings were confected by Florence the cook. In the dairy, old Mr Abbot churned yellow cream and a stiff salty butter more delicious than any I've tasted since. In the greenhouses, Tom, the head gardener, would, with tender, earth-blackened hands, offer us choice ripe strawberries and vine tomatoes perfumed like exotic fruit.

In London, we habitually ate a lot of bread and jam, Spam, Kraft cheese slices, Ryvita, toad-in-the-hole, tinned ravioli — parsimonious

4

post-war food which kept us very thin. Here at Linkenholt, we consumed roast grouse, honey-baked ham, rhubarb syllabubs, treacle puddings, apple pies and cream. And we could give our whole attention to these wonders. Nobody expected us to speak much at mealtimes. I think it was assumed that girls would have nothing to say. We just had to sit up straight and wipe our mouths nicely with starched linen napkins and, when the meal was done, ask Granny if we could leave the table. 'Can we get down, Granny?' we would say. But she would never answer. She would just give a furious little nod of her head, which made her powdery chins wobble.

Yet I don't think we cared. I can remember running straight out of the dining room, through the hall, down a long passage, past a locked gun room, to the back door where our bicycles waited. A circuit or two, perhaps, round the restless elms, then away down the drive, out into the ever-unfolding green spaces, through a larch glade, up a chalky hill, pushing our bikes towards a great wood of beech and fir, oak and ash, where pheasants were fattening themselves up for the shooting season. Or sometimes, if an excited, daring mood was on us, we would cycle slowly from the manor gates to the top of Linkenholt Hill, stop for a moment, then whizz at colossal speed, as fast as we could, down the hill, the scented hedgerows a blur, the bright sky seeming to bounce at the edge of our vision.

Skidding to a stop at the bottom of the hill, we might meet Mr Carter, the gamekeeper, with his posse of lively Springer spaniels. The dogs would come rushing towards us — five or six of them. Jo loved this rush. She would kneel and pet the dogs, while I ran away. Bred as gun dogs, they were, I'd always assumed, adept at biting things, and I imagined those things would probably include my limbs or my face. Mr Carter would gently encourage me to stroke the dogs, but I never lost my fear of them.

Mr Carter was a man of few words, who lived alone in one of the estate cottages, a house with a strange tower growing out of its roof. He always treated us with patience and affection. And this was true of all the people who worked for the Dudleys. We must surely have been annoying to them, ridiculous even — spoilt kids from London, charging about on expensive bikes, given every material thing we asked for. But, perhaps because they had lived through the tragedies that had so wounded the Dudley family, they understood why our grandparents were unable to give us much affection, and so they compensated by showing us what kindness they could.

The person we were closest to was Douglas Abbot, only son of Mr Abbot who looked after the dairy. Douglas had two roles, as butler and chauffeur. He was tall and very thin, with a gentle voice, never ruffled by our grandfather's outbreaks of bad temper. In a special cupboard in the dining room, he kept orange squash and ginger beer for us. Once, when with our cousins Jonathan and Robert we'd built a tree house in the spinney beyond the rose garden, Douglas Abbot climbed the makeshift ladder to our hideaway carrying four glasses of squash on a silver salver.

When I think about this extraordinary image, I understand that if part of your childhood is spent in a paradise like Linkenholt, a veil falls between your eyes and the truths you need to learn about the world. Later, this veil falls away.[1]

★   ★   ★

---

[1] In my first novel, *Sadler's Birthday* (1976), written when I was 32, when I was no longer 'Rosie' but Rose, the apprentice writer, I was making my own fragile amends for the social structures still in place in England in the late 1940s and 1950s. The book is about a butler, Jack Sadler, who inherits the big house, the 'Linkenholt' where he has once been a servant. The roles have been judiciously reversed. Yet such reversals can be distorted by the very people who benefit from them. Sadler finds that he's unable to lead a life mirroring that of his former employers. He can't lead it because he can't bring himself to *employ servants*. And so he suffers on two counts: he's intolerably lonely, and the house and grounds begin to crumble around him. He keeps himself alive by remembering his only loves: his adoration of his mother and his desperate, transgressive love for Tom, a London evacuee boy billeted on the house during the war. His world is full of ghosts. The only living thing to give him comfort is his nameless dog. He spends Christmas absolutely alone.

Christmas at Linkenholt involved beguiling preparations.

Every year, Jo and I were allowed to dig up a tiny Christmas tree from the spinney and keep it in a pot in our bedroom. (In January, it was replanted in the wood.) We decorated it with glued-together things: branches of wild oats, with the seed heads wrapped in multicoloured sweet-papers; pine cones and twigs dipped in glitter powder; garlands cut out from strips of chocolate foil.

We festooned our room with home-made paper chains and tissue-paper bells, bought from Woolworths in the King's Road in London. We gathered our toys around the tree: my pig and his two rag-doll friends made by me, complete with extensive wardrobe, and named Mary and Polly; Jo's dog Diggles and his companion Little Bear. We sat them up and let them marvel at our decorations. Mary and Polly put on their cocktail gowns.

Downstairs, in the library, the other tree, the real Christmas tree, waited. It was very tall and reached out its wide scented arms far into the room. Here, the decorations we loved most were strange pastel-coloured Victorian angels with anguished faces and long flowing gowns made of horsehair.

On Christmas morning, after the deep pitch darkness had sighed us to a long sleep, we woke to find filled stockings, heavy and rustling, on the end of our beds. We always opened these alone, instructed to let the grown-ups lie in (presumably after their Christmas Eve tippling).

The stockings themselves were the heavy wool socks Roland Dudley wore for shooting. The small presents were wrapped in tissue paper: chocolate cigarettes, tiny furniture for our doll's house, crayons, Matchbox cars, gobstopper sweets, packets of transfers, a tangerine in the toe . . . Then our mother would come in, probably smoking her first du Maurier cigarette of the day in a long black holder, to make sure we were washed and tidy for Christmas breakfast.

She was very particular about our hair. Jo's hair was insanely curly — 'beyond hope', our mother said. She could never figure out where this curly hair had come from. (We once annoyed her by suggesting that Jo was African.) My hair was just straight and slippery and had to be tied in bunches or clenched into obedience by a tortoiseshell slide, which kept falling out. She'd look us up and down. In some way that I can't quite fathom, we disappointed her. Had she longed for boys, inherited a 'boy only' love from her parents? Had she even lost a boy child in the miscarriage she'd endured during the four years between Jo's birth and mine? I will never know now. All I can remember was that this disappointment was of long duration.

★   ★   ★

Christmas breakfast was a fine Linkenholt moment. I can recall the sun coming through the mullions of the south-facing dining room, falling onto the mahogany sideboard, where Douglas would carve a ham on the bone and set slices

9

before us on fine china plates. In my household in Norfolk, when my daughter Eleanor and her family come for Christmas, we still eat ham on Christmas morning. Indeed, small remembered delights have been lifted from Linkenholt and brought into our lives and kept vibrant there. We now wrap the grandchildren's stocking gifts in tissue paper.

After the ham breakfast, we'd put on our best coats — the ones from Hayford's of Sloane Street, with little velvet collars — and walk to Linkenholt church, the place where I was christened and where Jo, given a candle to hold during the christening ceremony, floated off into one of her dreamy moments and set fire to her disobedient curls. Our grandfather would usually read one of the lessons. Granny never moved from her pew. She'd sit there, wearing a strange floppy velvet beret, staring at the arrangements of holly and ivy, her face unmoving. No doubt she was thinking of her dead sons. *In the bleak midwinter. O little town.*

St Peter's Church, Linkenholt, is a tiny flint building halfway down the single village street, set back against ancient yews, with a Germanic 'witch's hat' tower and a graveyard almost empty of people. When our grandmother died, Roland Dudley had constructed a lychgate in her memory. When Roland himself died, a second marble plaque was put into the gate, commemorating his life. When my mother died, I and my stepbrother, Sir Mark Thomson (always known in the family as 'Mawkie'), obtained the agreement of the vicar and the church wardens to add two more plaques, naming Jane and her second husband, Mawkie's father, Sir Ivo Thomson. And Jane's ashes, as she instructed, are scattered on Linkenholt Hill. A libation of Gordon's gin was poured on them.

Mawkie and I — together with my daughter Eleanor and my beloved partner of twenty-five years, Richard Holmes — still make a pilgrimage to Linkenholt from time to time, usually choosing the spring, when the hedgerows offer up primroses, violets and the small white flowers we used to call 'star of Bethlehem'. We walk up to the house to find it gated and locked, the gravel driveway now a tarmac road. The elms are gone, of course, but the spinney is still there and the wind still makes it sigh. I like these visits. I like seeing the ghost of Rosie in her feathered headdress, riding round the lawns on her Raleigh bike. But Jo has never been back there. She's a person who is able to put portions of her past into oblivion. It isn't that she can't remember them; she just doesn't want to revisit them.

Without Jo, I would have been lonely as a child at Linkenholt. The grown-ups mainly put themselves into a drawing-room existence, where they smoked and drank and played cards and did *The Times* crossword and waited for meals to arrive. Only Roland, who had worked as a civil engineer in India and now put all his energies into modernising and mechanising his huge farm, found this tiresome, and would bounce away down the drive in his old jeep, which he drove with alarming abandon, like Mr Toad, off to visit his sheep or his cattle, or to argue with

Mr Carter about which woods to shoot when. The dog, Jill, stood up beside him — his most favoured passenger.

Sometimes, after tea, he would take us with him in the back of the Land Rover — these strange little girls he laughingly called Rosebud and Jo-bags — to witness lambs being born, to admire the new bailer he'd invented for straw and hay, to watch stubble being burned. At first, we loved these outings. But one day, when we were riding with him on the combine platform, Jill came rushing towards us across the half-harvested wheat field. Jill loved her indulgent master. She didn't like being without him. She attempted to get to him by trying to climb up the rotating blades of the combine. I remember the stricken look on Grandpop's face, his shouted instruction to stop the combine and his call: 'Jill! Jill! My Jill!' But the dog kept climbing and was torn to shreds before our eyes. We never rode on the combine again.

\* \* \*

Before Christmas dinner, Jo and I put on identical dark red velvet frocks with lace collars. We were allowed to go down to the library and take fronds of silver tinsel from the tree to make pretend tiaras for our hopeless hair.

Next, we sat and waited for the servants to come in to be given their gifts by Granny; Douglas smart in a tail coat, Florence's cheeks scarlet from the kitchen heat, the housemaids always dressed in pigeon grey. What gifts did they get? Heartbreak hadn't turned the Dudleys into Skimpoles, so perhaps good money was handed out, or perhaps Douglas had been dispatched in the Rolls to Andover or Marlborough to find 'appropriate' items. But the servants' presents were never opened there and then. Everybody just stood around with glasses of sherry. There was a kind of awkward silence to these moments that nobody knew how to overcome. No doubt Michael Dudley, renowned for his good humour, for his jokes and his laughter, would have found the right things to say, but he was long gone.

After this, while Florence basted her vast turkey and Douglas put the finishing touches to the beautiful table, the grown-ups drank champagne. We drank ginger beer and opened our presents. There were few, but they were always good. The objects I remember loving most were a tin cash register, and a blue scooter, very like the ones all kids love riding today, but heavier and harder to steer. But what did we — polite children that we were — give Roland and Mabel? Something would have been organised: a 'shooting' tie for Grand-pop, Yardley's soap for Granny, hankies or talcum powder for eccentric Great-Aunt Violet, who some-times left the dark confines of her flat in Grosvenor Street to brave a Hampshire Christmas? I can't remember.

What I can recall is that Christmas Day at Linkenholt passed for us in an almost debilitat-ing haze of excitement and overeating. After the roast turkey and the plum pudding, after more ginger beer and Mint Crisps and crystallised fruit, Jo and I would climb slowly up the

13

green-carpeted stairs with the brass stair rods, tired out by sheer delight, our tinsel tiaras lost somewhere under a heap of wrapping paper. We'd get into our flannel pyjamas and stare out at the night and wait for the sound of the wind. We'd ask our toys if they had had a lovely day.

★   ★   ★

On Boxing Day, there was always a shoot. Grandpop had redesigned the Linkenholt acres with shooting in mind, planting beautiful woods and copses where the birds, so carefully bred by Mr Carter, could shelter and feed. We heard the *quark-quark* of pheasants all the time on our walks. Often they had lumbered into the air, panicked by our whizzing bicycles on Linkenholt Hill. Now the poor exotic creatures were driven from the woods and copses by an army of beaters and felled by the guns. The dogs seemed to shimmy with delight as they raced in to retrieve the bodies.

The men who gathered for the shooting party were the same each year, neighbours of the Dudleys, each with his own estate. Between them, this country elite must have owned about a third of Hampshire. They wore heavy tobacco-scented jackets, checked shirts and plus fours. The skin of their faces was ruddy and roughened by their outdoor life. Many of them had bristling nasal hair, which you hoped wouldn't touch your face as they bent down to give you an avuncular peck on the cheek.

But they were a friendly old bunch. The nicest

14

of them, Sir Eastman Bell, who owned Fosbury Manor, had developed a late passion for daffodils, and every Easter he would invite us to lunch, to walk with him round his acres of flowers. He must have had thirty or forty varieties, spreading out across lawns and fields and into woods. He didn't grow them to market them; he grew them because he loved them.

The Fosbury daffodils presented to me and Jo a sight we never, ever forgot. It surely outshone in variety and wonder the golden blooms that Wordsworth saw 'beside the lake, beneath the trees/Fluttering and dancing in the breeze'.

Time goes slowly when you're a child, and I used to imagine that those fields of flowers were still there all through the summer and into the first leaf fall. Later, I realised that Sir Eastman Bell spent two thirds of his year looking at drooping brown stems or bare grass. But he sacrificed the months of this empty landscape for his paradise of a spring.

Sometimes Jo and I, wearing woolly hats and gloves, stood with him for one of the shooting drives. He'd remind us about the need for silence as we waited for the sound of the beaters coming nearer through the woods. And the quality of this silence — men standing in line with guns, the dogs obediently quiet, a mist hanging low over the plough, or even a light snow falling — I have never forgotten. The images are almost like images of war, and yet what I felt, as a child, was wonder. It felt like a silence that contained all my life to come. My grandfather and his friends were somewhere near the end of their time on the earth, but what I could see was the landscape spread all around me in its winter magnificence, waiting for me to find my place in the world.

It could be bitterly cold out on the Linkenholt fields. But the cold was part of the wonder, an endurance necessary to the time. I remember curling up my freezing toes inside my wellingtons, holding on to Jo for the warmth of her arm. And once, Sir Eastman gave us a nip of cherry brandy from a silver flask — a river of scented lava creeping down inside me. He patted our woolly heads. 'Don't necessarily tell your mother,' he said.

Then the pheasants began flying up, making their honking cry, and the guns were pointed at the sky, and the russet and green bodies fell and the air was scented with cordite.[1]

★   ★   ★

I have often wondered, did Jo have this feeling of some marvellous existence waiting for her beyond the Linkenholt fields?

------

[1] In our childhoods, Jo and I were told the fiction that a great-uncle on our father's side, Jocelyn Thomson, had 'invented' cordite and, appalled by the deaths his own destructive invention had caused on the battlefield, later committed suicide. I have no idea how this lie went wandering through the generations. Cordite was alchemised by Sir James Dewar and Sir Frederick Augustus Abel in 1889.

For I grew up with the reality of Jo's genius. From a very young age, she was a seriously brilliant artist. Art teachers at school cooed over her. Our Aunt June (our father's sister), who was something of a painter herself, nurtured Jo's talent with frequent superlatives. Even our mother, who never liked to 'show off' by praising us, was aware that Jo was gifted and might have a professional future.

At Linkenholt, when rain kept us indoors, we began a little book together. It was called *The Bear who Went to Sea*. I can remember nothing about the story I wrote, but I can still see Jo's vibrant little pictures: the bear setting off with his knapsack; the bear discovering a sailing boat in a cove; the bear at sea, alone with the night, with the moon and stars, longing for home.

And Jo entered a national newspaper competition with a crayoned picture of me at Linkenholt. It was titled 'My Sister on the Farm'. I'm wearing my corduroy dungarees, a woolly jumper and a scarf patterned with windmills and Dutchmen wearing clogs. This picture won first prize (two guineas, I think) and was printed in *The Times*. Jo would have been no older than nine or ten. Even Granny thought this was terrific.

⋆　⋆　⋆

In the summer holidays, our cousins Jonathan and Robert were sent down to Linkenholt to be with us. Their mother Barbara, Michael's widow, had married again and given birth to two more sons, James and Charles. Roland and Mabel never

17

invited Barbara or the other boys to Linkenholt. I believe, in their immovable post-war snobbery, they had never much liked their daughter-in-law, whose father was a Jewish businessman, Bertie Stern. Perhaps Barbara had never seemed good enough for their beloved Michael. And now they never saw her or her new husband. When summer came around, they snatched their grandsons from her and put them in Jane's care.

Johnny and Rob had (and still have) an affection for our times at Linkenholt as fierce as mine and Jo's. But I remember our mother complaining about having to look after four kids instead of two. Later in our lives, she told us that while she knew that we and the cousins were 'in paradise' on these holidays, she was 'in hell'. It was the hell of feeling unloved, of arguing with Grandpop over trifles, of enduring Mabel's unending, debilitating grief.

And perhaps the presence of the boys didn't help her. They were noisier and larger than us. They adored climbing trees and riding their bicycles through puddles even faster than we rode ours. Their clothes got muddier. And, most importantly, they were less afraid of Jane's bad temper. They slept in a room across the landing from ours, where, Rob complained, the birds kept them awake all night. Jo and I would often emerge from our tranquil sleep to hear Jane shouting: 'Will you boys BE QUIET!'

They didn't want to be quiet. Linkenholt was a paradise for them too, and the expressions of their happiness could sometimes be noisy. Johnny's nature tended somewhat towards anxious obedience; he was a boy who wanted to please. But Rob, I think, didn't care much what any of the grown-ups felt about him. He was perpetually lively and restless and would keep talking for as long as anyone would listen. And he had a wonderful knack of saying things that made everybody laugh. He became the house jester, as Michael had allegedly once been. Even Granny's cross mouth would stretch itself into a secret grin at some of Rob's sayings and antics. And to see Granny smile — a thing she did so very infrequently — was a strange phenomenon, as though, for a moment, a different personality had taken her over.

She loved it when the boys sang to her. Before lunch, sometimes, when the grown-ups were on to the sherry and we would be ravenously hungry (after a morning spent playing in the garden, trying to climb hayricks or building dens in the spinney, but cleaned and brushed up by Jane), we would cluster in the drawing room and Johnny and Rob would sing, in their sweet boy-soprano voices: 'The Minstrel Boy', 'Molly Malone', 'Oh Shenandoah' . . .

What worlds of memory did these songs evoke in Granny? Had Michael once sung them, or poor little Roland? It interests me to recall that, as far as I can remember, Roland was never talked about. He must have died in about 1926 — thirty years before. So did the sheer weight of time cast some oblivion on him? Or had he perhaps been a weak boy, of whom Roland and Mabel were very slightly ashamed, whereas Michael had been large and loud and strong?

And when Mabel looked at Jonathan and Robert, who did she see? I like to think she saw these children only for who they were — these deeply individual souls — but I fear the ghost of one or other of the dead sons hovered always round their heads. Robert had a tomboyish look, laughing brown eyes, hair wild, clothes slightly out of order. Jonathan was tall, athletic and beautiful. He was, to some extent, their 'golden boy', but his young life was made difficult by a debilitating stammer, brought about, it seems, by the tragic loss of his father.[1] Rob, who had no such affliction, managed to steal their hearts with his jokes and his laughter.

---

[1] In Johnny's short book *Winston, Churchill and Me*, about his friendship with young Winston Churchill, grandson of the Great Man, he recounts a fearful moment at Chartwell when Sir Winston asks him (he is eight years old) what he's going to do when he grows up. Having really no idea what he's going to do, he embarks on a 'first big consonant, an F', planning to say that he might be a film director. But he can't get the words 'film director' out. Churchill tells him gently to take his time. But time doesn't necessarily help stammerers. They are in real psychic pain. They have to latch onto the first word they can manage to say. Johnny finally blurts out that he'd like to be 'a fishmonger' when he grows up and registers in Churchill's eyes 'a deep boredom, an ennui so implacable there was nothing for it but to retreat to my chair and hope that I would never have to speak again'.

I don't remember that Jo and I were ever invited to join in with the singing sessions, but I'm pretty sure we didn't mind. The cousins brought fun and daring to paradise. We loved them. We only tried to puzzle out, I recall, what on earth or *where* on earth was Shenandoah.

★ ★ ★

Johnny and Rob were quite skilled at tennis, and Jo and I, already given tennis lessons at the Hurlingham in London, were good enough to play children's mixed doubles with them, all of us tutored by Jane, who kitted herself in a white pleated skirt, white plimsolls and white-framed sunglasses. She was thin but strong. Her high-kicking serve could sometimes take even Johnny by surprise. Tennis was one of the few activities she deigned to engage in with us.

Above the tennis court was a summer house, where Granny occasionally came to watch us play and keep murmuring, 'No, no, no . . . ', as though everybody was doing everything wrong. The summer house was full of cane furniture, once brown and shiny, now faded to lichen grey and slowly dismantling itself, like sinews falling from dead bones. Granny laid herself down on these bones and stared at us and at the wrecked tennis court, its asphalt blackened and broken apart by weeds, its chain-link fencing rusting in the sun.

We once asked Jane why, when everything else at Linkenholt was kept in such pristine order, the tennis court looked like something from an urban slum. But we probably knew the answer before we asked the question. 'Michael,' she said. 'Michael loved to play tennis. Now, no one plays.'

We played. But who were we? I suppose we were the 'no ones'.

★   ★   ★

But we were real to many others.

One of these was Mr Daubeny — a neat and energetic man with, ironically, the physical colouring of a fox — who cared for the chickens.

The coops were set out over two grassy fields. Mr Daubeny used a pony and cart to make his rounds of feeding, watering and egg collecting. This pony and cart was so beguiling to us, I used to dream about riding in it. But I think it was Rob, also fascinated by the idea, who eventually plucked up the courage to ask Mr Daubeny if we could 'help' him. He said yes. And so, instead of just watching Mr Daubeny work, we gained access to all the paraphernalia of caring for hens: untying great bales of straw to spread fresh in the coops, rounding up birds that had escaped into prickly hedgerows, searching for eggs, topping up the grain feeders and the water troughs. We were farmers at last.

We probably caused more chaos for Mr Daubeny than he ever admitted, but he seemed happy to let us follow him, bundling us all into the cart as we moved from one part of the field to another, and — miraculous event! — letting one of us ride *on* the pony as we went.

If we went there towards the end of the morning, we would get to ride down to the farm buildings where the pony was fed and stabled at lunchtime — over the two fields, down a chalky track, then onto the road, where in the 1950s almost no cars ever came, but which gave us a wild feeling of excitement and daring. The road was steep and narrow, with tall hedges on either side. Once, we met a Green Line bus and everything came to a standstill. Did we turn the pony and cart around, or did the bus back away down the hill? I can't remember. I just recall that Rob was riding the pony, and when he saw the bus, he let out one of the expletives that used to blue the air in conversations between Grandpop and Mr Carter.

Then we'd trail back up the hill to the house. Did one of us own a watch, or did we just tell the time by the hunger we felt or the positioning of the sun? As I recall, none of the grown-ups showed any anxiety about us. Perhaps this is one of the excellent laws of paradise: that time is no longer an enemy, but a watchful friend, steering you home before anybody misses you, before any rule has been broken.

We went pounding in, remembering to take off our wellingtons at the door, our cheeks long cured of their London pallor, our clothes pricked here and there with bits of straw and feathers. Jane would lead us away to the bathroom, perhaps complaining that she was missing her third glass of sherry, that we stank of chicken manure. In her slender hand would be a hairbrush.

When I was nine, our grandmother fell ill.

Children were not told the names of serious illnesses in those days. We only knew that Granny had taken to her bed.

Douglas and the maids came and went with cups of broth and glasses of Sanatogen. It was winter. The cousins weren't there to sing to Granny, so Jo and I were taken into her suite of rooms, to stand quite far away from her and try to remember the words of 'Oh Shenandoah'. This wasn't a bit of the house where we ever normally went. But I remember finding it beautiful, painted in soft greys, with a grey carpet and ornate cherrywood furniture the colour of honey.

Granny had stomach cancer. Grief, cigarettes, sherry, arthritis and overeating had made her body slightly grotesque. Now she seemed shrunken — a different person. She looked at us sadly but intently from her mound of pillows. She said she would like to hear 'Rudolph the Red-Nosed Reindeer'. It was as though she'd noticed us at last, knowing she wouldn't have to be bothered by us for long.

Jo and I were strangely disconnected from the idea of her death. Johnny remembers Granny as a kindly person, much liked by all those who worked at Linkenholt. But we didn't like her very much. My most tangible memory of her was when, walking along the lavender walk with us, she would lean on me, to steady herself, and the weight of her hand, pressing down on my shoulder, would get heavier and heavier until I wanted to scream with pain, but knew that I couldn't.

Apart from this remembered torture, surrounded by the lavender-scented air, I think Granny had never really been fully alive for us, just a cross, ghostly presence who had given us a paradise to inhabit and then withdrawn from it.

The one macabre gift we had from her, early in our visits, was a plait of red hair that had been hers when she was young. Jo seized on this, attached it to her disgraceful curls, covered them with a scarf and pretended to be Deborah Kerr in the hit movie *King Solomon's Mines*, which we'd already seen two or three times. I was thus press-ganged into spending a portion of my childhood attempting to impersonate Kerr's co-star, Stewart Grainger. Later in my life, I got to know Frankie Shrapnel, a horticulturalist, wife of the actor John Shrapnel and Deborah Kerr's daughter. Frankie, too, had beautiful red hair. She was very amused that I'd spent so much time facilitating the imaginary world of a person who sometimes believed herself to be her mother — or 'DK', as Jo liked to call her.

Looking back at Granny's dying, I understand that Jane was crucified by the approaching loss of her mother. If you haven't been loved by a parent, you never quite give up on it — even though part of you knows that you should. You obstinately keep hoping that he or she will somehow *discover* this affection before they die. And then, when they're nearing their end, you realise that it's never going to come, that their afterlife you carry in your heart will be as arid and as lonely as the lived years. I think the overwhelming feeling in Jane was fear. She dreaded being left alone to cope with her father.

Granny didn't die at Linkenholt. She died in a London hospital, where I know we were taken to see her not long before she vanished out of our existence, though I have no recollection of the visit, only the memory that we'd missed out on tea and that I was terribly hungry. We rode home from the hospital on the Tube, whereas our habitual mode of transport in London was the buses — the 19, the 22 and the 137. I remember seeing how all the cigarette stubs, thrown down by the Tube travellers, had collected between the wooden slats of the floor, and how everybody stared at everybody else as we flew through the darkness.

# Cast Away

We didn't know it then, but on that Tube journey we were beginning to speed towards an altered future.

Granny's death was the first alteration. It changed the character of our visits to Linkenholt. Jane and Grandpop argued at mealtimes. Sometimes she ran out of the dining room, slamming the door. Grandpop just carried on eating, as though nothing had happened, giving morsels of his food to the new spaniel puppy, also named Jill. I think all Jo and I could do was sit very still, frozen to our chairs. This was the world we'd entered now, a world where nothing was happening, nothing visible, but under the surface, massive tectonic plates of feeling were shifting. We were headed for the storm which swept us away.

⋆   ⋆   ⋆

Until I was ten, our lives followed an unvarying pattern. We lived in a small house at 22 Sloane Avenue, in Chelsea (a pleasant but ordinary little London borough then, not the outlandishly expensive place it's become since the 1960s), and attended the Francis Holland School in Bourne Street.

Every morning we walked to school with our nanny, Vera Sturt — past the bomb site at the end of the road, past Pritchard's the bakers, where you could buy a loaf of bread for fourpence-halfpenny, past Boots, with its lending library at the back of the shop, past the barrow boys selling fruit and flowers, past the newsstand where we were allowed to buy our comics, *Girl* and *School Friend*, to read when we got home.

Vera Sturt, or 'Nan' as we called her, was the anchor in this London life. I shared a bedroom with her. She wore slippery floral nighties, bought from D. H. Evans in Oxford Street. She said her prayers kneeling silently by her bed. She smelled of coal-tar shampoo and talcum powder. She brushed my hair with great gentleness. She and I threw bread to the birds that wandered on a flat roof beyond our tiny window. She was the kindest person I've ever known.

Nan got us up in the morning, made us porridge or toast for breakfast and took us to school. In the afternoons, she collected us and either brought us home to play and read in the nursery before tea, or took us to Chelsea baths for a swimming lesson, or else brought a picnic tea to eat in Cadogan Gardens, where we played on the swings and Jo, mesmerised by a pretty child from Paris who also played in the gardens, pretended to be French. Her adopted name was Antoinette.

We then walked home with Nan: Antoinette and Rosie, who was sometimes dragooned into being Antoinette's English friends Daphne or Di, or both at once, whose main task was to praise

28

Antoinette's clothes and the fine ribbons she wore in her sumptuous hair.

Before bath time, we were taken down by Nan to see the parents, Jane and our father, Keith Thomson, in the drawing room. Waiting to enter this hallowed grown-up space, Jo stopped being Antoinette and usually stood behind me at the door, pushing me forwards into the room as though suddenly afraid to be herself again and present that face for scrutiny.

Keith Thomson was a playwright. He worked in a study on a half-landing, the walls hung with posters from his productions. We grew up with reverence for his work, hearing his typewriter clacking, always remembering to be quiet on the stairs, because 'Daddy's writing'.

But his career had been marked by disappointment. The plays had never made it from provincial theatres into London. The one that had at last been commissioned by a West End theatre, *Out of Sight*, was cancelled when its star, the then famous Margaret Leighton, bowed out of the production to take the lead role in a film titled *I Want to Live*. And the whole body of his work would soon become unfashionable and meaningless to the British public as his type of 'drawing room comedy' was superseded by the realist, angry plays of the new wave — by John Osborne, Arnold Wesker and David Storey. Realising, perhaps, that his future as a playwright was now uncertain, he took up an offer to direct the York cycle of mystery plays at the York Festival and disappeared up north. He cast as his

Virgin Mary a then unknown young actress called Mary Ure.[1]

As many writers do, Keith used his work as an excuse not to join in many family things. There is one photograph of a family picnic in Richmond Park, and I can remember him being at Linkenholt for one or two Christmases. He played the Blüthner piano in the Linkenholt library, smiling as he played, as though his own talent amused him. He was a quiet showman and encouraged us all — even Granny — to attempt complicated costumed charades. But he was a man who was easily bored, who found that the people around him at this time in his life didn't entertain him enough. He was fond of his sister, June, who dabbled in painting, and he had some slightly bohemian friends in London, whom he liked. The Linkenholt Tory shire culture, however, was anathema to him. On Boxing Day, he would drive back to London to escape the pheasant slaughter. Even Sir Eastman Bell's acres of daffodils wearied him.

How unhappy or discontented was he at this

---

[1] Keith always claimed to have 'discovered' Mary Ure, who went on to star in the film version of John Osborne's *Look Back in Anger* (1959) and other high-profile movies. But perhaps she had already been discovered. Perhaps she just liked the idea of playing the Virgin Mary and so agreed to work on the mystery plays for a brief season. We were told so many untruths by and about Keith Thomson that I no longer know precisely what was true and what was a fiction.

30

time? Jo and I saw him so little, we had no real idea who he was. He almost never took us anywhere or played with us on his own, as though he were afraid we would suddenly need something he didn't know how to give.

He was a small, neat, dark-haired man with an amused, ironic smile and large, tired brown eyes, who had fought in the war in Germany and survived, but who had come home to children he barely knew. He'd met Jane while he was still at Oxford and she'd come over from Linkenholt with some friends to see one of the OUDS plays, in which he must have starred. Women always adored Keith, so he probably had other girlfriends before deciding to marry Jane in 1937, when they were both twenty-four, but these young women are lost in time.

There used to be a picture of the recently married couple in the drawing room at Linkenholt, one of those old soft-focus photographs that yields up its detail only slowly. The brightest bit of the picture is Jane's bouquet of arum lilies — now more usually associated with death. She wears a slim, silky dress and white gloves. The faces betray almost nothing — neither happiness nor fear. Yet I know from things she told me long after Keith had abandoned her that Jane always saw him as the love of her life. What he felt about her I've never really known.

And what did we, his daughters, feel? Perhaps we loved him primarily because our access to him was rationed. Spending time with him had to be regarded as a treat. If he wasn't actually absent from us, in his study, or away somewhere, he would often *seem* absent, his head engaged too deeply with his writing or with the other feelings that were stirring in his life. The thing he liked doing best on his rare visits to our nursery was to read our comics aloud. The names of the characters made him laugh: Belle of the Ballet, Lettice Leefe, the Greenest Girl in the School. But he would never stay long. Nan called him 'Daddy' (just as she called Jane 'Mummy'), as though her voice, addressing the parents, was ours and ours alone. 'Stay a bit longer, Daddy,' she would say. 'Read one more story.' But he never would. There was always something that called him away.

His work in York on the mystery plays earned him a surprising OBE. For this to have happened, his production must have been startlingly good. But we were never taken to see it. We just waited for him to come back. But in one sense, he never came back. Nothing was said or known until later, but in York he'd fallen in love with a much younger woman, Virginia Wood, who'd worked with him on the production.[1] He and Jane were

---

[1] We'd been told that Virginia Wood was our father's secretary in York, but years later, when I dropped the fatal word 'secretary' into a newspaper interview about my childhood with John Walsh in *The Sunday Times*, a ton of unlooked-for fury came screeching at me from Keith's household in Kent. I was accused of 'insulting' Virginia. I'd recently sent my father a copy of my 1993 novel, *Sacred Country*. This was returned unread. And as far as I know, none of my subsequent novels were ever read by him.

both aged forty in 1953. Virginia — it later emerged — was twenty-five. We didn't know it yet, but he was lost to us.

The last time I see him clearly in my childhood is at Buckingham Palace, wearing a tail coat, smiling at the young Queen, crowned that very year, as he was given his honour. He was the smallest man in the line. Above him reared the red-and-gold caverns of the Throne Room. (Jane worked out that the enormous height of the ceiling would mean that the drop on the chandelier above us would take it from the chimney of our house to the pavement below.) Keith trod the deep-pile carpet lightly, in narrow black shoes. The smile on his face was, of course, a secret one, only half there for the new Queen. It was the smile of his new-found happiness.

⋆   ⋆   ⋆

People in love are ruthless, and Keith handled his leaving of us badly. It seems he made one attempt to come home and save his marriage, but he wasn't able to do it. In the end, he and Virginia just ran away together.

Jo and I were told nothing for a long time. When many weeks had passed, we begged Nan to tell us where he was, and she, who was always uncomfortable with lies, said she thought he might be 'in the north again', working on a new play. People came and went from the house in the evenings. As we sat by the nursery fire, listening to *The Mill on the Floss* on Nan's wireless, we sometimes heard Jane crying.

More time passed. Poor Nan was forced back on untruths more than once: 'Daddy will be home soon . . . He's got a lot of work to do . . . He's in Germany . . . '

Then the day came when the grown-ups decided that everything had to be revealed. I was ten years old. Nan made tea at elevenses time on a Saturday morning. It was raining outside. The little gas fire in the nursery popped and flickered. Jane came up, wearing dark glasses. Jo and I were given milk and chocolate biscuits.

Nan had to tell us because Jane couldn't get the words out: our father had gone away for ever. He wasn't in Germany. He didn't love us any more; he loved someone else. Life was like that sometimes. We just had to bear it.

The nursery furniture was painted pale pink. We sat at our pink table and tried to work out what exactly there was to be borne. I remember thinking that it was a shame the typewriter would be so silent. And then there was Lettice Leefe. What would become of her without the gift of my father's amusement?

We didn't cry. Jane wept and clung to Nan. We just sat there, saying nothing. Perhaps we were thinking that life wouldn't change much without Keith, because he had hardly ever spent any time with us. Perhaps we imagined that everything would just go on as it had always gone on: the walks to school, the picnic teas with Nan, the buying of comics, the listening to the wireless by the fire, the swimming lessons, the visits to Linkenholt . . .

But we were wrong. All of this was about to be snatched away.

★ ★ ★

It's the endeavour of most abandoned wives to keep their children close to them when their world collapses, but Jane — even with Nan's affectionate help — couldn't cope with us.

We were taken away from the Francis Holland School — away from our friends, from the games of rounders in the playground, from the warmth and guidance of good teachers, and worst of all, away from Nan — and sent to a little-known girls' boarding school, Crofton Grange, in Hertfordshire.

What was Jane *thinking?* I was not yet eleven years old, and Jo was fourteen. We were both hard-working kids who had thrived at our London school and made many friends. But our mother's life was in ruins. She needed to be left alone to try to put it together again. With us gone, Nan was no longer needed. She, too, was sent away — to live with her sisters in their small house in the village of Dogmersfield in Hampshire. The pink furniture of the nursery stood abandoned. Aside from Jo, who was caring and affectionate towards me at Crofton Grange, I knew only one girl, Jane McKenzie, whose parents followed our mother's example in dispatching their girls to a distant academy.

Jane McKenzie and I had met at Miss Vista's dancing class at the age of three. At a Christmas show entitled *Meadow Flowers*, the two of us had been cast as 'thistledowns'. We wore little cotton slips, with skirts of billowing white net into which pieces of cotton wool had been sewn.[1] Did we feel stupid, or proud of how we looked? I can't remember. I think we may have been too young to care. Jane was blonde and blue-eyed and sweetly pretty, so she probably felt better about herself than I did. Who knows? All I know is that Jane McKenzie and I became very close friends at this early, slightly embarrassing moment in our lives, and that this friendship lasted until we were grown-up and our lives diverged.

★　★　★

Meanwhile, the grown-ups in London were playing musical beds. With Keith gone, and Jo and me safely dispatched to Hertfordshire, Jane embarked on a love affair with our father's cousin, Sir Ivo Thomson.

---

[1] Though I've seldom drawn directly from my own life in my fiction, in *Sacred Country*, I have a 'thistledown' scene. Six-year-old Mary Ward, who lives with the conviction that she's really a boy and embarks on a long, arduous journey to change gender, is enrolled in dancing classes, which she despises. At the Christmas show, orchestrated by a teacher also named Miss Vista, Mary is due to come on as a thistledown, but sabotages the event by appearing in her wellingtons. After the show, her father takes her outside and beats her.

Ivo and his wife (always known as 'Tweets'), Jane and Keith and another couple, Brian and Vera Whitmee, had been close friends in Chelsea. Now, Jane began sleeping with Ivo and Tweets began sleeping with Brian Whitmee. How they contrived these affairs, in plain sight of each other, I've never completely worked out. But it was as if abandonment had become contagious. Once Keith had led the way, the others seemed to wake up to the idea that, although the war was quite far in the past, the 1950s was yielding a drab and constrained life from which only something as electrifying as brand-new love would deliver them.

Mawkie later told me that he suffered real and lasting agonies over his parents' divorce. He'd been informed of it in a letter, sent to his prep school, Sunningdale, by his mother. Aged twelve at the time, Mawkie kept this letter for years and years, as though he feared these were the last words his mother would ever say to him.

And in a sense, he was right: they were the last words she would ever say to him while she and Ivo and their two children were still a family. Mawkie and his sister Carol, as well as Jo and I, were kept right out of the grown-ups' emotional arithmetic, almost as though we didn't exist.

They kept us out, perhaps, because they knew they were behaving in a wild kind of way. They took their new love brazenly, where it was the least trouble to find, among their closest circle of friends. Only poor Vera Whitmee, who came from Poland and dyed her hair a strange reddish-purple colour, appeared to be left out.

Keith had Virginia, Jane had Ivo, Tweets had Brian, but Vera had no one. I believe she must have clung to her only child, Sophie, who had sometimes been invited to tea with us. She had been a child who tested Nan's eternal patience, a girl with an angry face who sometimes stamped her feet and sent our toys skittering over the nursery linoleum. But I think she may have been her mother's only consolation. Later, when we worked out how things had happened during this time, I began identifying with Vera Whitmee, imagining her in some distant freezing landscape, cast out, as we were cast out into boarding school, never completely understanding where her previous life had gone.

Tweets, on the other hand, was serene. She was a very beautiful woman, of whom Jo and I (and Nan) had always been slightly afraid. She had once come up to our nursery to use it as a space in which to change for dinner, and we had marvelled that the dress she climbed into, wearing oyster-coloured silk underwear, stood up on the floor of its own accord, like some throwback crinoline. We never forgot this: Tweets being helped to mountaineer into her frock. She seemed to disappear inside for a moment, then rise out of it, like a witch emerging from a shimmering circle of flame, with her wide mouth smiling and smiling — smiling and smiling. I remember that, unkindly, I didn't want her to smile. I wanted her to go away down the stairs and leave us alone.

That Tweets left Ivo for Brian seemed strange to me. Tweets and Ivo had always been a mesmerisingly handsome couple, perfectly designed for each other. But something had gone wrong. 'After the war,' Jane once said, 'nothing was ever the same again. You children simply didn't understand.'

So Tweets turned to Brian and Ivo turned to Jane. Brian was a man I remember as being strangely inert; he had one eyelid that drooped, as though in perpetual apology for the goings-on of the time. But it turned out he was phenomenally rich. He married Tweets and they lived in grand London houses for the rest of their lives. The space I saw in my mind in these places was always Tweets's dressing closet, with her sumptuous dresses waiting on padded coat hangers, great ranks of them, made of silk taffeta and brocade. I imagined Tweets caressing not Brian's droopy eyelid, but the exquisite texture of the dress fabric.

★　★　★

Ivo was a fun-loving man, fond of verbal jokes and puns, who'd had a comparatively easy war on the ground in the RAF, so had retained an obstinate boisterousness and careless optimism. At the time he began his affair with Jane, he'd recently retired from a director's job with the York Herald Newspaper Company, which owned the *Yorkshire Evening Press*, selling his shares in the *Evening Press*, for enough money to start his life afresh.

Keith had driven a Hillman Minx. Ivo drove a Bentley. If Jane's heart had been broken by Keith (as she said, all her life, that it had been), Ivo successfully wooed her with jewellery and nylons and dinners at the Berkeley — and no doubt with the confident passion of a good-looking man, and the irresistible tickle of a tiny little moustache he kept fastidiously trimmed. 'I was helpless,' she later said to me. 'I tried to get away from Ivo, but I couldn't.'

Everything was done terrifyingly fast. During our first holiday from Crofton Grange, when Nan was invited back to look after us once again, we thought some portion of our old lives would return — our little routines with the swimming baths, the picnics in Cadogan Gardens. But we were wrong.

The day came quickly when Nan once again set out the tea things for elevenses, once again braced herself for news of change escaping from bottled secrecy. So up Jane came to the nursery, to the chocolate biscuits and the tea, but this time she was smiling. It was winter, and cold in the room, and Jo and I were sitting on the hearthrug, near the gas fire. And then she told us: she was going to marry Ivo, and Ivo was buying us all a house in the country. Our lives in London, in our house, so sweetly regained in this brief holiday, were over.

That was when we cried. Both of us had been mute at the news of our father's departure, but now, at the idea of our mother as the wife of Sir Ivo Thomson (our 'new father'), we began to howl. Nan got down onto the rug and put her arms round us. Jane looked on in dismay. Then she began to cry too. She cried, I think, because

40

she realised for the first time — perhaps for the only time, because she always resisted emotional analysis — how much had already been taken away from us, and how impossible it was for us to feel happy for her. The grownups had entered a period of sexual madness, quite beyond us to comprehend. And now, to Jane's shock and dismay, the reality of that madness was being put to judgement by our unstoppable wailing.

She tried to console us with promises: Ivo would buy us a dog; we were going to live in a country house by a river; Mawkie and Carol would become our siblings and friends; everybody would soon get used to everything . . .

We clung to Nan, hysterical with fear and sadness. 'Mummy darling,' Nan said eventually, in her calm, untroubled voice, 'perhaps it's better if you go downstairs for now.'

★　★　★

That night, my eyes hurt. To try to relieve the swelling and the ache, I began to tug out my eyelashes, one by one. I must have looked like a weird albino monkey.

# Mother

My mother had been sent away from Linkenholt to boarding school — St Monica's in Buckinghamshire — when she was six years old; two years younger than everybody else at the school.

How had this come about? Had St Monica's been bribed to take this hapless little girl? How did they, or my grandparents, imagine a child of six — whose education up to that time had been sporadic, presided over by a lazy governess — was going to cope in a class of eight-year-olds?

Jane told us that she couldn't cope at all. She just sat at the back of the classroom 'not understanding a thing'. The teachers seemingly couldn't be bothered, even, to learn her first name, and called her 'Little Dudley'. She was so homesick and unhappy, she couldn't eat, but she was made to eat and then she was sick. She was sick almost every day. She got so thin and weak, she was dumped in the school sanatorium for weeks on end. My grandparents never visited.

Surely Charles Dickens in his blacking factory can scarcely have been more miserable than my mother was at this young age? If Jo and I felt like outcasts when we were sent to Crofton Grange, I can't begin to imagine the pain in six-year-old Jane's heart at this terrible childhood banishment. And I think it's true to say that, emotionally and to some extent physically, she never quite recovered from it. I now have a six-year-old beloved grandson, Archie. The idea that any comparable exclusion from the family could be inflicted upon this beautiful, vulnerable child makes my blood turn to ice.

Jane said that the only thing that gave her 'hope' was the coat our grandmother had bought for her before she left. She said it was a beautiful little coat, lined in silk, with a short cape sewn into the collar seam and covering the shoulders. Jane reasoned that if her mother cared enough about how she looked to buy her this expensive coat, then that might be proof that she loved her — 'at least a bit'.

I never saw this precious garment, this supposed emblem of a mother's affection, but it has always seemed clear to me that Mabel Dudley loved nobody on this earth (including my grandfather) except her two sons. At the time she sent her daughter away, her elder son, Roland (who was soon to die), was at Harrow, and no doubt she missed him. I can only believe that it irked her to give house room to Jane when Roland was forcibly absent; better, in her selfish mind, to get rid of Jane and leave the adorable Michael, then aged four — too young for school of any kind in those days — as the only child, to be spoiled and petted at home.

It was at this time, at St Monica's, made miserable by being called 'Little Dudley', that Jane decided to change her name. She had been christened Viola Mabel: Viola, perhaps, after Shakespeare's feisty heroine, or more likely — in a philistine household that nevertheless took pride in a beautiful garden — after the sweet pansy flower, and Mabel after her mother.

But she didn't feel that either of these names belonged to her. Nobody at the school could pronounce Viola properly. Once they'd abandoned 'Little Dudley', they began calling her 'Vi-oh-ler', which Jane knew was ugly and wrong. And it was difficult for her to live up to 'Mabel' — to try to be like the mother who had sent her away. So she made a decision. She explained that 'All my life I'd been told that I was plain, so I said, right, I'll be 'Plain Jane' from now on and that's what everyone must call me.' She kept the V.M.T. initials for legal documents and chequebooks, but she was Jane to her family and friends until the day she died.

I've always admired her for this. She got her way. She understood that names are important, that you need to own them and feel that they fit the person you imagine yourself to be. Throughout my childhood, I was always called 'Rosie'. The name just followed me along, except at school, where I was 'Rosemary' (my given name) to most of the teachers, and at Linkenholt, where I was often 'Rosebud' to Grandpop. But I never felt comfortable with any of these names, and I can sometimes conceive of my childhood as a long journey towards the one-syllable noun I could properly own: Rose. Just as Jane, from the age of seven or eight, refused to answer to Viola, so I, from the age of twenty, refused to answer to Rosie.[1]

*  *  *

It is from the St Monica's time that my mother's struggle with food can be dated. At Linkenholt — as I experienced as a child — the food from the farm and the vegetable garden, beautifully prepared by Florence and her helpers, was nourishing and abundant. Jane knew how good food should be cooked, and when she married Keith, she took herself on cordon bleu courses to learn how to do it. My father mocked these endeavours as the 'strain-in-champagne-and-throw-away' school of cookery, but this was unfair. Having been through the war and its aftermath of rationing in England, my mother, though keen to acquire new 'professional' skills, hated waste in the kitchen and was always clever at finding ways to use up leftovers. Jo and I grew up with fond memories of her recycled lamb shepherd's pies, scented with fresh sage.

---

[1] Naming is important to many of the characters in my fiction, never more than to Mary Ward, in *Sacred Country*, who believes, from the age of five, that she's the wrong gender. The name she chooses for her male persona is Martin, and when someone recognises her new identity and addresses her as 'lad' for the first time, she is overwhelmed with joy. 'It was as if,' she says, 'the whole of existence is paid for in some way, except for that one moment, which is free.'

Jane's real trouble was that she thought she loved food. She talked about it eagerly, greedily. She certainly loved it in her mind, but her body was almost perpetually in rebellion against it. The sickness she'd endured at St Monica's followed her throughout her life. Sometimes she vomited in the middle of a meal. Her rush from the room was something we came to dread but had to get used to.

In consequence, she was as thin as Wallis Simpson, and like Wallis, prided herself on this lean body shape, this almost-flat silhouette, and on the exquisite clothes it could slip into like a shadow.[1] She despised fat people. And she wanted Jo and me to be modest little reeds of girls. At puberty, we were made to wear elastic girdles, 'because nobody wants to see the cheeks

---

[1] Wallis Simpson, so vilified in the British press, has always been a figure of fascination to me. Discovering how harsh and punishing both her upbringing and her first marriage were, I wrote a short story, 'The Darkness of Wallis Simpson' (2005), revisiting some of this difficult past, which is never considered when moral judgements are passed upon her, because so few people know about it. The story turns on the provoking idea that in old age, a prisoner of her Paris apartment, Wallis can remember the deprivations of her youth and her marriages to Win Spencer and Ernest Simpson, but has forgotten every word about her history-altering marriage to England's Edward VIII.

of your bottoms under a skirt. That is a quite disgusting sight.'

There was so much in the world that disgusted her. She once told me that cleaning her teeth made her feel nauseous. How she got on with sex with either of her husbands, I don't know. At the time of her first marriage, she'd had to go into hospital for an operation to make her vagina wider to accommodate my father. Perhaps this narrow, clenched vagina was quite stimulating and exciting (again, as it was reputed to be in Wallis Simpson's body), and kept my father by her side until he found somebody he truly loved and who loved him back.

Jane had no schooling in love. She had never been given it — except a little, perhaps, by her easy-going, sweet-natured brother Michael — and so she didn't know how to feel it or how to show it. This was the tragedy of her existence.

Near the end of her life, she kept desperately repeating that she loved me, and she certainly had a deep affection for three (but only three out of seven) of her grandchildren: Jo's eldest son, Guy, her elder daughter, Kate, and my only daughter, Eleanor. But these protestations came too late to be believed. Love needs words and deeds to be perceived as love, and Jo and I grew up entirely without the feeling of being loved by our mother. We skirted round her moods and furies like the undernourished cubs of a wild she-wolf. We crept away to Nan's comforting lair, where the sound of her voice was sweet and calm.

As an antidote to her struggles with food, Jane

chain-smoked. She inserted du Maurier cigarettes into a black holder from Dunhill's of
Mayfair, which contained a filter that captured
some of the tar. From time to time she would
change the filters, and I can remember clearly
the sight of the little plastic oblongs, sticky and
brown, which she told us saved her lungs from
becoming congested by tar.

But the word 'tar' always bothered me. In the
1950s, a lot of municipal tarring was going on in
London, as cratered roads were repaired and
new pavements laid after all the destruction of
the Second World War. Jo and I liked to watch
the giant steamrollers pressing this pungent,
treacly substance into the earth.

I particularly remember one tar engine,
moving back and forth at the end of Walton
Street, outside a fishmonger who sold live eels,
shiny and black as the tar, in white pails. Ever
since, black eels and molten tar have always been
associated in my mind, as though the tar might
have emanated from the eels' bodies, a lava of
petroleum-scented caviar, bringing London back
to life.

But the idea that some of this same
suffocating, burning roe could end up inside my
mother felt strange. This is one of the troubles
and the wonders of childhood: you imagine
things wrongly. And later, when the truth is
known — assuming there is an absolute truth
— the unwinding of the imagined thing is
tangled, because the first image keeps on
obstinately breaking through. You're adrift in
mystery and ambiguity. And yet for a writer's

imagination, the unfixed place is sometimes a promising place to dwell. Black eels and tar; a caviar of tar in my mother's thin-chested body: these are absorbing images. When Keats presented his enabling concept of 'negative capability', he was reaffirming the creative power that 'uncertainties, mysteries and doubts' can provide.

Now and then, I experienced the du Maurier tar first hand. There was a game Jane and I occasionally played, when I was eight or nine, in which I would pretend to be her and she would pretend to be me. My essential prop was the black Dunhill cigarette holder. I would stick this between my teeth and taste both the tar residue and the Chanel lipstick that always smeared the end of it. I would sit on a sofa with my legs discreetly crossed, doing pretend smoking, and then pick up the telephone to dial the speaking clock, then known as TIM, talking back to it in 'Jane language': 'Darling. How are you, darling? Are you, darling? Are you really?'

Jane, in her turn, would mime eating sweets and dropping the sweetpapers all over the floor, and I'd order her to pick them up and she'd do pretend crying. Then, with surprising athleticism, she would walk round the floor on her hands (a feat I'd perfected in the Francis Holland gym), and her skirts would sometimes fall down over her body and I'd see her elastic girdle and her suspenders and stockings and her expensive knickers from Harrods. And all of this would always make us laugh.

I remember that I felt closer to her during this game, in which our identities were hilariously swapped, than at any other time in my childhood. We were teasing each other, for once, and this gave us a kind of equality of status. I remember one day when we were both lying on the sitting room carpet, giggling unstoppably, my father walked in and said, 'What is this? Did Lettice Leefe drop by? Don't tell me I've missed her?' And he joined in the laughter and the sound of it was beautiful.

★   ★   ★

Why could there not have been more times like this? Why was Jane so often perched on an abyss of anger with her girls?

One day, when I was six or seven, she took me with her to Liberty's to buy some dress material. While she was paying for her fabric at the pay desk, housed just outside the department itself, I found myself mesmerised by a free-standing display cabinet, made of wood and glass and resting on spindly legs. The cabinet was full of buckles, and the thing that fascinated me was the idea of a buckle without a belt — as though this object might suddenly have multiple uses of which I'd never dreamed. I think I must have gone into a kind of buckle trance. The next thing I was aware of was an immense shattering sound, as of a bomb being dropped, and then I saw that the whole cabinet had fallen and lay in a thousand shards on the wooden floor.

I stood there in shock. I didn't, at first, understand that by leaning on the cabinet to gaze at the buckles, I'd knocked it over; I

50

thought something else must have happened: a rocket had come down from the ceiling or a wicked genie had surged out of the floor.

Jane began screaming at me. She told me I was a thoughtless, clumsy 'idiot child'. She said she would have to pay a ton of money to Liberty's to compensate them for the broken cabinet and it was all my fault. So then I saw that I'd done something worse than anything I'd done before in my life, worse than breaking the bell on my bicycle, worse than not waiting for Nan at a road junction on my scooter, worse than refusing to wear a hated blue mackintosh to school. I was lost to my own awfulness.

I screamed so hard, I think the customers downstairs in the gifts department must have heard me. I screamed so disturbingly hard I lost the ability to breathe. I imagined that anybody hearing about this crime would hate me as Jane seemed to hate me, so the thing I began to babble was 'Don't tell Nan! Don't tell Nan!' And this, no doubt, was the last straw for Jane — that I should dread so much the idea that Nan would think me bad. So she hit me, *whack!* on my ear, and I fell backwards against the Liberty's panelled wall.

Sales assistants from the fabric department came running. The next thing I was aware of was a kindly-seeming woman kneeling by me and holding out to me little miniature swatches of material. She pointed out the different colours, the different patterns. I can see them still, these swatches. Cotton and silk and chintz and damask. And I can still feel the warmth of this

51

person, her hand on my arm, her voice gentle like Nan's. Little by little, I stopped screaming, and I remember turning and seeing the staircase going down towards the street, and the carpet on the stairs was green, the exact colour of the hearthrug in the nursery. And I thought only about being back there, with the gas fire flickering blue and Nan sitting in her armchair doing her knitting, and voices on the radio.

*Maggie Tulliver, come away.*

★   ★   ★

All through our London years, before the great Casting Away, we spent part of our summers at a house in Cornwall, owned by the Trusted family, on the dunes above Constantine Bay.

Mrs Trusted, or 'Auntie Eileen' as we were instructed to call her, was one of Jane's best friends. She was as broad and jolly as our mother was thin and anxious. She cooked enormous egg-and-mushroom pies for us to take on beach picnics. She called Jane 'Janet' and I remember that I liked the sound of this name, as if it would, in time, alter Jane and make her kinder.

The Trusteds inhabited a sprawling stuccoed house on a windy point. They stayed there all summer. When we visited, the house contained only women. There was Auntie Eileen, her daughters Susan and Sarah-Jane, and their nanny, Gladys, known as 'Glad Eyes'. Then there was Jane and Nan and Jo and me. Neither Mr Trusted — Johnnie — nor our father ever came on these holidays. But there was one male presence: Eileen and Johnnie's youngest child, their son Timmy.

Timmy Trusted was a pretty blond boy, the darling of his mother, the apple of Glad Eyes's beady eye. Everybody loved Timmy except me. He was almost exactly my age, so I was expected to play with him. We played chasing games over the dunes, but he could always outrun me, and this was how I came to regard him: as a boy who would always be ahead of me, in every race and in every game and in the hearts of the grown-ups. He wasn't like my cousins, Johnny and Robert, who sang beautiful songs and just joined in things and didn't need to win all the time. Timmy, aged six or seven, already knew his own power, and I suppose I reinforced this by trailing after him.

But I couldn't find any other companion. I was stuck with Timmy and he was stuck with me. Jo and Susan Trusted were close friends, and Sarah-Jane, two or three years older than me, preferred being with them. Even the nannies, Nan and Glad Eyes, got along well, while Jane and Eileen smoked and drank and laughed and boiled hams and made crumbles in the kitchen. I remember lying in my room feeling sorry for myself, longing for this holiday to be over, longing to be at Linkenholt — an Indian chief once more, not a sulky squaw.

There were moments of strange delight. It was Glad Eyes's task to collect all the bread crusts and leftover cake that was thrown away in the household and feed this to the seagulls. The ritual went like this: Glad Eyes put all the food in

53

a big enamel tin, walked to the end of the garden, then banged on the tin with a wooden spoon. I used to marvel that even before she had started hurling out the bread, a great screaming, wailing flock of gulls would appear in the sky and then descend — in numbers worthy of Hitchcock's film of Daphne du Maurier's *The Birds* — onto the lawn at her feet. It was like a terrifying magic trick. In minutes, the gulls pecked and gobbled all the bread and cake and took off once more into the air.[1]

Then, of course, there was the sea and its shoreline of deep rock pools. In Treyarnon Pool, we lined up to dive from a slippery flat rock. I can still feel the fear and excitement of these dives, the thrill of the icy water. This was a different universe from Chelsea baths, dangerous and wild, with the screech of seabirds above and the sea crashing in just over the headland.

---

[1] In a very early short story, 'Wedding Night' (1983), this image is one of several I use to recall the lost childhood of my twin French protagonists, Jacques and Paul, whose English mother dies when they are fifteen. She came from Cornwall and recalls for them sitting on a wall watching her father banging a tin full of bread, then 'surrounded by the seagulls, by the chaos he had caused'. Part of what the boys have lost, in their sophisticated life with their French father in Paris, is the wildness of their maternal homeland. I felt that the gull scene illustrated the character of this wildness — and the anarchy that is part of it — strangely well.

We learned to surf in Constantine Bay. My surfboard had a picture of a dancing seal on it. We got bolder as time went on, taking our boards further and further out, till Jane and Eileen came and stood at the edge of the water, calling us in, and Eileen's Pekinese dog joined them, barking at the waves and the wind.

In the wet sand left by the receding tide, Jo led us all in making sand sculptures. Hers were beautiful: mermaids with realistic fish-scale tails and Botticelli hair, seabirds with spread wings. Mine were lumpy, sometimes starting out as known animals and ending up as creatures nobody recognised. And it amused Timmy, who thought sand sculptures girlie and stupid, to jump on mine and break them apart. When the weather was too bad for diving or surfing, we were consigned to a playroom housed in some kind of annexe or garage and almost entirely taken up by a ping-pong table. Timmy was, predictably, good at ping-pong. He used to hit the ball so hard, it bounced away into the jumble of cast-off things: broken deckchairs, golf clubs, hammocks, cardboard boxes, old thermoses and gin bottles. We'd spend as much time looking for the ball as playing. And boredom lay heavy on these days of storm.

★ ★ ★

One summer, the circus came to St Austell.

Auntie Eileen bought tickets for us all and we counted the days to this moment of thrill and cruelty. None of us had ever been to a circus, but

55

we knew that there were going to be lions, and trapeze artists dressed in spangles, flying through the air. We knew that the lions might escape from their cage and maul the ringmaster. We knew the trapeze performers might fall. In our heartless children's dreams, we *wanted them to fall*. It promised to be the most exciting thing any of us had ever seen.

Then on the morning of the St Austell day, I was summoned by Jane. She told me that I wouldn't be going to the circus after all. I wouldn't be going because I'd been 'difficult'. I had to learn to fit in better and be nicer to everybody, including Timmy. If I didn't learn this lesson, then my life would not really amount to a life. I would be no one.

I slunk away, crying, to the room I shared with Nan. Nan told me she'd go to 'Mummy' and plead for me. Telling me I would be 'no one' was, in Nan's vocabulary, 'rotten'. Yes, I had been cross and sulky. Even the kindly Glad Eyes had complained about me. But Nan understood that staying in this friendless household was difficult for me, so she'd go to Mummy and Mummy would relent.

But Mummy didn't relent. Everybody went off to see the man-eating lions and the death-defying acrobats, and Nan and I stayed behind. Nan was missing the circus too, but of course she didn't complain. She was a person who hardly ever complained about anything.

For our supper, we had boiled ham and bread and butter with salad cream. And the following morning I woke up to find a scarlet mess all over my pillow. I thought I'd been weeping blood, but it turned out that a vessel in my nose had burst — a tiny red mark on my face I'd had for years and which, on the night of the circus, had exploded. When Jane saw me the following morning, all she said was 'Why does Rosie look so pale?'

★   ★   ★

Although Jane and Auntie Eileen presided over our Cornish holidays, almost all our out-of-school activities in London were done with Nan. The one exception was riding lessons.

These were organised for me and my friend Jane McKenzie by our mothers when we children were eight or nine. They took place in Wimbledon, and I can remember that Jane McKenzie and I travelled there in the back section of the Morris Traveller and annoyed the mothers by staring backwards out of the little lumpy car and making ugly faces at the motorists behind. This behaviour the parents described as 'dreadfully common'.

At first, I looked forward to the riding lessons. I liked my outfit: yellow polo-neck jersey, trim jodhpurs, little tweed jacket, yellow gloves, a velvet-covered riding hat, a whip. I felt privileged and thrilled.

The hot, sweet smell of horses was alluring to me, and their beauty has always struck me as exceptional. But mastering them takes courage and strength, and the paths we rode on Wimbledon Common were stony and uneven, full of places where the horses might slip or slide. At Linkenholt, when Jo and I and the cousins took it in turns to ride Mr Daubeny's pony, I'd felt no fear at all, only colossal excitement and joy, but now, in Wimbledon, some agitation about falling off and breaking my neck started to creep into my mind. This increased as we progressed to learning to jump, a feat I felt proud of doing and yet was definitely afraid of.

Jane McKenzie was a neat and competent rider; I was told by my mother that she had 'a very good seat', and the memory of her rod-straight little back going up and down on her horse is a tender one. In contrast, I was informed that I looked 'like a sack of potatoes', that I lacked *spine*. This classic put-down, coupled with my increasing fear that riding would somehow end my life, should have been enough to stop me continuing with the lessons. But I wanted to keep up with Jane McKenzie and the other children at the riding school; I refused to admit my fear to anyone, even to Nan.

Over time, this bravado became an increasing agony to me. I would wake on the morning of the riding lessons feeling sick. When we went into the stables to lead our horses out, the sweet scent of them would now be tainted with the smell of terror.

It was, in the end, about five years later that I told my mother I didn't want to go on with riding lessons any more. Knowing nothing of the fears of her spineless sack of potatoes, she had no sympathy to give. I just remember her complaining that it had all been a colossal waste of money.

★ ★ ★

Before our lives in London ended, something happened between me and Jane that directly concerned money.

This series of events has always remained a mystery to me, a mystery that makes it harder than ever for me to understand why Jane was the kind of mother she was.

One of our grandmother's sisters, Marie Michell, a rich eccentric who lived with a female companion in a cavernous house in Norfolk, had agreed to be godmother to me. We hardly ever saw Marie Michell. Jo and I were taken out to tea at the Hyde Park Hotel from time to time by another of the unmarried sisters, Great-Aunt Annie, and the youngest of the siblings, Great-Aunt Violet, once or twice turned up at Linkenholt for Christmas. But Marie had her own woman-centred life at Kenninghall; she wasn't remotely interested in our family or in godmothering. My birthday was never remembered. At Christmas, sometimes a hated box of handkerchiefs would arrive, *With love from Aunt Marie*. And I was made to write 'a proper letter of thanks' to her. But mostly, she just chose to forget us all.

Then, on my tenth birthday, just before Keith left us, a cheque for £100 was sent to Jane by Marie, to be spent or saved for me, acknowledging that Marie had not been a good godmother

59

and hoping that this would make amends.

This was 1953. A hundred pounds was a large sum of money then, too large — obviously ridiculously too large — to be given directly to a ten-year-old child. So I was summoned by Jane and told that with a little of the money she would buy me a new bicycle (I had now outgrown Jo's cast-off Raleigh), and the rest would be 'put somewhere safe' for me, to have when I was grown up.

We bought the bicycle: another Raleigh, shimmering blue, with a new chrome bell. It was a good machine and I loved it and kept it for years and years. The sum I think this cost was £14 or £15, thus leaving £85 to be put into the promised safe-keeping.

I forgot about this money. Great-Aunt Marie probably forgot about it too. But years later, at a time when I was struggling financially in my twenties, I suddenly remembered it and asked Jane if it had been invested for me — in a Post Office savings account, perhaps? I realised that £85 would have transformed itself into a much larger sum in the twelve or thirteen years that had passed, and that this might conceivably relieve my financial stress. But no. Jane admitted that she had just taken the rest of the money and used it for herself, seemingly without a qualm. 'I'm sorry, Rosie,' she said to me, 'but I'm afraid Aunt Marie's money coincided with a difficult time for me. You had your bike. I honoured that. The rest just *went*.'

*It went*. It was mine, but Jane never seemed to care about what was mine. (In a later house

60

move, she threw away all my teenage letters, all my school reports bar one, and a collection of my early poems.) She cared that Jo and I would be honest and upright in our own dealings, but in so many ways she was dishonest and cavalier, both with the things that belonged to us and with our feelings.

It came to me in later years that she *envied* us. We hadn't been sent away from home at the age of six, with nothing but a beautiful coat to keep our hopes of love and affection alive. We hadn't gone through the war. We hadn't known what it was like to lose not one but two beloved brothers. And we'd had the luxury of an affectionate nanny — paid for by Jane. We were a thousand times more fortunate than she had been, and it was as if, in her arithmetic, she decided: *Jo and Rosie have got quite enough already, thank you very much! I endure Linkenholt for their sakes. I fill their Christmas stockings. They don't need me to make financial sacrifices for them. They don't need me to love them.*

I think that when we were around her, she didn't feel as though she was living. We made too many childish demands on her. She had to have hopes and expectations for us, which wearied her. As girls in a man's world in the 1950s, what could those hopes and expectations possibly be? And if she thought them up, then she'd have to begin worrying that we might not fulfil them.

When we were safely away in our cold dormitories at Crofton Grange, she and her friends could forget all about their children's future. Instead, they could go to plays, go to films, go to restaurants, get drunk at lunchtime, flirt, shop, swear, take taxis, waste money, go dancing, have sex, and wander through London in the dawn light, laughing, determined to forget the war that had stolen their youth and so many of the people they'd loved. They were making up for lost time. With disintegrating marriages, they knew that life was slipping by for them, but that for us — the bloody children! — it was infinite. We had years in an apparent peacetime wonderland ahead. It wasn't fair.

A friend of Jo's, Lois Crane, who later became head girl at Crofton Grange, told me some years ago that her mother had witnessed a distressing send-off scene at Liverpool Street station, where we assembled for the train taking us back to school. My mother and Pam McKenzie dutifully kissed my friend Jane and me goodbye, ignoring any weeping that might be gathering in us, then, before the train had left the station, linked arms and turned away, saying, 'Good! Now we can get on with life!'[1] But what was that life? A roll-call of the things I've listed above, ending with the

---

[1] This image has great power in my mind. I didn't witness it, but I can see it and hear it very clearly. In order, perhaps, to exorcise it a little, to make it less painful to me, I used it, virtually verbatim, in a short story called 'The Closing Door', in my collection *The American Lover* (2014). In the story, I punished the woman who is most like my mother. I took her husband away from her and left her with an unknown future.

London daybreak shedding a harsh light on all of them.

It has always felt to me that my mother's generation of women, born just before the First World War and suffering painfully through the Second, had been dealt a difficult hand. Those who survived well bucked the constraints imposed on their aspirations and found purpose and sanity through work. But Jane was not one of them. Her greatest human weakness was to care a lot about the way people *looked*, but to be too emotionally and intellectually lazy to attempt to understand what they *felt*. Heartbroken as a young child, she cursed, drank and chain-smoked her way through a life that passed in a kind of peculiar, pampered dream, unexamined, never completely understood.

# Angel

She was one of eight children, two of whom had died young. The six who remained were Sissy, Madge, Lilian, Judy, their brother Colin, and Vera, our beloved Nan. Sissy was a widow. None of the other sisters had ever married. Their father had been a family doctor and left them each a little money. Two of them found work in nursing. Vera became a nanny. Early in my life, she said to me: 'Never do this. Whatever happens to you, don't become a nanny. It's too heartbreaking.'

Before coming to us, when I was born in 1943, she'd worked for another family and doted on her charge, little Peter Taylor. But when Peter got older, she was no longer needed. Nan mourned for this lost child. She had to begin all over again with us. Peter Taylor was twelve and at boarding school. Instead of him, Nan was faced with dreamy, curly-haired Jo, aged four, and baby Rosie, rather plump and prone to dribbling.

Until the war ended, we lived in a small cottage, David's Cottage, on the Linkenholt estate. (It's here that I locate the memory of lying in my pram and seeing birds landing on telegraph wires.) There is a photograph of us all, including Great-Aunt Violet, taken on my first birthday in the garden of David's Cottage. I appear to be holding a tiny book, or perhaps somebody's wallet or diary. Jo looks down at me in distaste: who is this fat baby who cries in the night and already shows off in the daytime? Cousin Johnny looks on in bemused wonder. Cousin Rob, not even one yet, is held up by his nanny. It's a summer's day, 2 August 1944. Jane has her famous white-rimmed dark glasses on, but Granny wears a coat and hat. Nan, in a white blouse, has her back to the picture, which was taken, presumably, by Barbara, Johnny and Rob's mother.

Of course there are no men there. Michael Dudley and my father were fighting in France. Were either of them thinking about us on my first birthday? Who knows? They knew, or presumably *hoped*, that we were safe. During the Blitz, a bomb fell on the corner of our road in London but spared our house, and now we were far removed from London. And our wartime life, because of the proximity of the Linkenholt farm, was never a desperate, hungry one. As the men suffered and died, we were gathered on rugs and in deckchairs in the sunshine. My bet is that Jane had made cucumber sandwiches for tea — the cucumbers grown in the Linkenholt greenhouses by Tom. And I was as safe as I was ever going to be. I was near to Nan.

★  ★  ★

At the Harbourfront literary festival in Toronto in 1991, I met the South African fiction writer Carolyn Slaughter, who was training to be a psychiatrist. Over lunch together at a seafood restaurant (with hilarious plastic bibs tied round our necks to stop us spilling lobster thermidor sauce over ourselves, and glasses of Chablis in our hands), we both began talking about the past.

Disarmed by Carolyn's revelations about being abused by her father at the age of six,[1] I eventually began telling her things I never normally discussed with anyone: the lack of love I'd had from my mother and father, and my emotional dependency on Nan.

Our lunch lasted hours. The Toronto sun went down at the window. And I have never forgotten what Carolyn said to me in the course of it. She reaffirmed very forcefully to me something we all now know to be true: that any human life, if the childhood is devoid of adult love, will almost certainly be a troubled one. She reminded me that it doesn't have to be the parent who gives this love; it could be an aunt or uncle or grandparent, or indeed a hired nanny. It just has to be *someone*. I was crying by this point in the conversation, but Carolyn reached out a hand and said: 'Crying is good, Rose. Use the big table napkins, but, hey, don't get lobster in your eyes. And listen to me: you were lucky. You could have been a depressive mess by now, or you could be dead from drugs or drink, but you're not. Nan saved you. She was your angel.'

---

[1] It took Carolyn a long time to begin to talk openly and publicly about her father's abuse, but she eventually wrote about it in a vivid memoir, *Before the Knife: Memories of an African Childhood*.

* ★ ★

Nan took us on our first great foreign adventure, to Wengen in Switzerland, in the summer of 1950, when I was seven and Jo was eleven.

Our parents were in the South of France, where they went every summer, and they presumably felt slightly guilty at the idea of abandoning us in smog-bound London while they sunbathed and danced and drank on the Riviera, or else they decided that some mountain air would breathe fresh life into us — that they might *like* us more when we returned.

I can remember snatches of the long journey: Nan getting down onto the station platform at Basle to buy food (there was none on the German train) and Jo and me calling to her from the window, terrified the train would leave without her.

In the evening, a steward came round with pillows and blankets and we lay down on the hard leather benches and tried to sleep, but sleep was difficult, for inside the pillows was straw, which rustled whenever you moved your head. I remember folding Piggy's floppy ears over his eyes, which was how I imagined he liked to sleep, and wishing I was a stuffed toy, who didn't mind about the rustling straw. In our compartment, there was a tiny blue light, which stayed on all night.

The final trains must have been from Bern to Interlaken, then from Interlaken to Wengen, where porters waited in the sunshine with carts drawn by St Bernard dogs. In the distance was the great peak of the Jungfrau. We had never seen a landscape like this one. The highest we'd ever been before was Linkenholt Hill.

Now, we were halfway to the sky, in a place where the war hadn't trespassed. My most vibrant memory of that first trip to Switzerland is the *shine* on everything: on the snow-clad mountains towering over us, on the red geraniums planted in a hundred window boxes, on the water of the hotel swimming pool, on the tin tables of a tea room where raspberries were served with a sour-tasting cream (probably crème fraiche), and — most tenacious of all in my memory — on the blue-black carapace of a stag beetle, sunning itself on a white road.

On one of our early walks above the Hotel Alpenrose, where Nan, Jo and I were sleeping in one 'family room', we discovered an old sawmill, where nobody was working any more but where piles of logs and planks lay strewn around among long grass and wild flowers. This became our favourite playground. We invented slalom games and balancing games, running in and out of the piles of planks and along the tops of the fallen fir trunks. It was high up, near the forest line, a strangely secret place that we soon felt belonged only to us. No other children ever came there.

At the forest edge, where Nan loved to watch for birds and kept hoping she would see an eagle, she discovered a lush growth of wild strawberries, a tiny fruit we'd never seen before. And I can still remember, in that bright Swiss air, with the sound of cowbells in the distance, the taste and texture of a wild strawberry, sharp yet sweet, scratchy yet soft. Perhaps Nan rationed them, because they always seemed precious and exceptional to us, as though we were eating jewellery.[1]

Aside from the sawmill games, we spent a lot of time jumping in and out of the hotel swimming pool, wearing our ridiculous rubber bathing hats, uncomfortable ruched swimming costumes and blow-up water wings. We took my dolls, Mary and Polly, for walks, suitably dressed in their Brownie uniforms, which I thought looked a bit Swiss. We talked pretend Swiss-German and made up words that made Nan laugh. We were given a little money to buy tiny Swiss flags and wood-and-elastic bracelets in the shape of edelweiss flowers, which we wore for years and years. We petted the St Bernards owned by the luggage porters and longed for a dog of our own. We contracted diarrhoea from eating too many raspberries.

One day, we took the funicular train up to the first stop on the Jungfrau and marvelled at finding ourselves in the snow in the middle of

---

[1] In my novel *The Gustav Sonata* (2016), a pivotal scene takes place on the edge of a forest in the Swiss Alps. My protagonist Gustav and his beloved friend Anton discover an overgrown path leading up through the firs. 'Wild strawberries were growing at its edge, tiny points of red, like beads of blood among the bandages of green leaves. Gustav and Anton stopped to gather a few of these and eat them. The texture was rough, but the taste was sweet.'

summer. We stayed up for supper in the hotel dining room and sang songs to Nan before we went to sleep: ('Barbara Allen', 'Kelvin Grove', 'Silent Night'). Years later, when Nan was dying (in 1964, the year I finally got to university), she remembered this singing; our children's voices carried out beyond the room into the mountain dusk.

★ ★ ★

Back home in London, we resumed our school routine.

We'd both learned to read early, helped by Nan and by the Francis Holland School's emphasis on reading and writing. Jo, whose bedroom was reached by a strange little passageway, running behind what Jane called the 'nursery bathroom', used to enjoy tucking herself away in there 'for a lovely read', and I can vividly remember lying on the nursery hearthrug and reading the books of Joyce Lankester Brisley. I never connected emotionally with her highly successful Milly-Molly-Mandy series, but adored her *Adventures of Purl and Plain*. Purl and Plain were two little wooden dolls, named after homely knitting stitches, with hinged legs and arms, pointy noses and painted-on hair: 'At first sight the two dolls seemed as if they might be rather prim and proper. But they weren't. They just loved adventures. They were as pleased as anything if they could fall out of the window or into the coal-bucket.'

What I liked most was how huge the world seemed to Purl and Plain and how familiar things, seen through their eyes, could become exotic and provide them with the adventures they never ceased to long for. For them, the hearthrug was a jungle, the bath a ski slope and knitting needles their ski poles. The attic was a terrifying universe, full of mousetraps, which risked breaking their legs. They could make a meal out of fried apple pips, but also wanted to be 'artists in cooking', confecting soup out of a drop of milk, green and red watercolour paint, candle wax and blue and yellow beads.

Precisely because these stories were rooted in familiar things, which could, in the imagination, become other things, I preferred them to *Alice in Wonderland*, where I was being asked to believe in grotesques, or even sympathise with their baffling antics. It has always seemed to me that for the novelist, it is a harder (and more grown-up) task to imagine the real world afresh, making it seem both familiar and yet new, than it is to imagine goblins or elves or even people made out of playing cards. I read *Alice* with Nan and our edition had illustrations by John Tenniel, which I eventually came to admire, but as a child, I could never *care* much about Alice. I remember thinking, I'm really glad this bossy little girl with her hair band and her sticking-out dress isn't in our rounders team at school . . .

What else did we read with Nan, sitting by the nursery fire? We loved things that made us laugh: A. A. Milne's poems from *Now We Are Six*, especially 'The Old Sailor', about a shipwrecked mariner who is so overwhelmed by the tasks he might undertake to save himself that he just gives up on all of them and waits to be rescued. I always used to make sure I was the one to read the last stanza:

And so, in the end, he did nothing at all,
But basked on the shingle wrapped up in a
shawl.
And I think it was dreadful the way he
behaved —
He did nothing but basking until he was
saved.

'Nothing but basking' I thought was a wonderful phrase. I used to imagine my parents doing 'nothing but basking' on the Riviera. When we were in Cornwall with the Trusted family, Jane and Auntie Eileen seemed to do nothing much but bask, while we ran in and out of the sea with our surfboards or tried to compete with Jo's beautiful sand sculptures.

Nan admired Robert Louis Stevenson's *A Child's Garden of Verses*, written in 1885, which she told me had been a favourite book of Peter Taylor's and must have reminded her of her life with him, now lost to her. I can remember her reading 'The Land of Counterpane' to me when I was ill — which I quite often was, probably after walking to and from school every day through London's terrible smoke-polluted air:

When I was sick and lay a-bed,
I had two pillows at my head,
And all my toys beside me lay
To keep me happy all the day.

I remember feeling worried that the boy in the poem had more toys than I did. The child has 'ships in fleets' and enough little houses to 'plant cities all about'. Perhaps Peter Taylor had also had toy soldiers and model houses? Perhaps his 'land of counterpane' had been complete in the way that Stevenson liked it to be, in a way that mine could never match?

All I had were Piggy, Mary and Polly, some pretend plates of food made of papier mâché and some doll's house furniture and two tiny occupants of the doll's house Jo had named Ebb and Flo. Ebb and Flo were made of pipe cleaners, and could be bent into any attitude of delight or despair that one chose. I also had a torch and could contrive Japanese shadow plays on the walls with the dolls. And I worked at my 'Knitting Nancy', a device made out of a cotton reel and four nails onto which you wound some wool, looping it round and over the nails with a crochet hook in some cunning way to make a woollen rope that began to come out of the bottom of the reel like a tiny snake. These snakes you could fashion into 'useful mats for grown-ups', the kind you hoped your mother might use to stand her glass of water on at night.

After my mother died in 2001, as Jo and I were sorting out her house, I found a little mat, made in pink and yellow wool on my Knitting Nancy, never used, I think, to stand a water glass on, but carefully tucked away with some old photographs in a drawer. I presume Jane had concluded that the colours were wrong for the decor of her room, looking too much like a

Battenberg cake to be displayed. Yet she hadn't thrown it away. She, who threw so much away, had kept this. Perhaps she remembered all the hours of work and dropped stitches that had gone into it?

★　★　★

I can recall how time stretched out eternally when I was ill as a child, as if a minute had taken onto itself some heavy burden that prevented it from moving past itself and on. When I read 'The Land of Counterpane' now, I can summon this up, this feeling of being held in a strange, dreamlike limbo — in a place almost as dark and subject to alteration as Alice's Wonderland.

The word 'counterpane' I always equated not with a proper bedcover, but with the green eiderdown on my bed in London. In my novels, in which eiderdowns — mercifully long superseded by duvets (except, I am told, at Balmoral, by order of Her Majesty) — occasionally feature, they are never described as being any other colour than green. Indeed, it's hard for me to imagine that they could be any other colour than green, for this is what I see in my own 'land of counterpane': my bed by the wall, papered pink, torn by me in places, to try to make words and pictures with my fingernails; Nan's bed, ready for the night, with her slippery nightdress spread out. A bedside table on which stands a tiny clock and my torch and the book, from Boots library, that Nan was reading at the time, probably a novel by Pearl S. Buck.

I move round my room in my mind and I see Nan's little dressing table with her Mason Pearson hairbrush and a saucer of hairpins, then a plain white wardrobe, in which, in winter, we forced hyacinth bulbs in china bowls in its useful darkness. And then the window, facing north, with some thin curtains, also green, and beyond the window, the flat roof, where the pigeons and sparrows gathered under the great secret canyon of the back walls of a 1930s block of cheap flats, Nell Gwynn House. I used to imagine that nobody saw this part of Nell Gwynn House but us. I presumed it wasn't meant to be seen, because this was where — from the dimly lighted windows — Nan and I sometimes heard people screaming and crying.[1]

I arrive back at my bed. I am in it, with my arms resting on the green eiderdown, but Nan is not there. Nan is having an evening off, spent with her cousins, Mary and Emmy, in Battersea. I am alone with my trio of toys, keeping as quiet as I can be, so that I'll be able to hear Nan's key turning the front door latch, two floors down, and know that, once again, I am safe.

---

[1] I was interested to discover, from Michael Holroyd's amusing and moving memoir *Basil Street Blues* that in the 1960s he had written his first major biography — of Hugh Kingsmill — in a room in Nell Gwynn House. The tiny flat cost him £3 per week. I have never yet asked him whether other residents of the building disturbed his work with their shouting or crying.

★ ★ ★

I think I was about six when Nan took Jo and me to Brighton for the day. The idea was probably that we breathe some seaside air, but the day was cold and windy and so we retreated from the freezing beach to a small fairground, where Nan bought us candyfloss.

After a ride on the carousel, and looking longingly at the dodgem cars but not being allowed to go on them ('Darlings, I think Mummy would be cross if you rode on those. You might bump your heads, or get your nice dresses in a tangle, you see?'), we saw a sign for a fortune teller and persuaded Nan to pay the sixpence to have her fortune told.

She went into a tiny booth, screened by a curtain, and Jo and I waited outside, trying to imagine all the amazing things that could happen to Nan in the future, like getting to meet the King and Queen or winning the football pools. But when she came out, we were dismayed. Nan told us that it had been predicted she would shortly go away 'on a long journey'. Jo began to cry. Nan soothed her by saying that fortune tellers were 'just pretending to know things'. But why, we reasoned, would anyone pay sixpence to be told things that weren't true? How could we be sure they weren't true?

From that moment, we were terrified by the idea of this 'long journey'. We knew it couldn't include us. And sure enough, a few months later, Nan was called away. Her sister Judy had broken her leg, and Lilian, with whom Judy shared a house, was recovering from a long illness. Nan had to go and take care of them both. We had no idea how long she would be gone, or indeed if she would ever come back.

Jane and our father no doubt conferred and discussed their own ability to look after us for a while. Could they manage it, with the help of the live-in cook, Mrs Hughes (known as 'Hughesie'), and the daily cleaner, Mrs Warburton? I've often imagined the conversation:

'Hughesie will help,' says Keith.

'Don't be silly,' says Jane. 'Hughesie can't possibly get our late breakfast *and* do the walk to school.'

'I could do the walk to school,' volunteers Keith.

'Don't be silly,' repeats Jane. 'You've never ever *been* there. You don't know where it is.'

'Yes I do. It's somewhere past the newsstand in Sloane Square where they buy their mag with Lettice Leefe in it. Have you read the Lettice Leefe picture story? The whole idea is actually quite amusing.'

Jane ignores this and asks: 'Who will get their tea?'

'Well, you could. It's only bread and butter and Marmite, isn't it? Or Hughesie will get it.'

'And who will put them to bed?'

'I suppose Hughesie will.'

'Don't be silly,' says Jane for the third time. 'You're asking too much of Hughesie. Then she'll get ill and there will be no more boiled tongue with caper sauce.'

'Oh,' says Keith. 'Well that puts a spanner in it. No caper sauce, eh? I suppose we'll have to pay for a new nanny.'

77

She was called Nanny Collins.

She was a thin, anxious woman of about fifty-five, with eyes that stuck too far out of her face and hairs on her chin, like some creature in *Alice in Wonderland*. In the night, lying next to me — just that tiny distance from my own bed — she snored and growled.

Jo and I cried and sulked. Jane sent for us and told us we were being unkind. Nanny Collins was a 'perfectly nice woman' and we were behaving like spoilt brats.

I think we tried to be better. We refused, still, to hold her hand on the walk to school. I began sleeping with a pillow over my head. But we let her read to us and put her scratchy face on ours, to kiss us goodnight.

In secret, however — shown only to Jo — I began a series of drawings of grotesque people, and I know that these were born out of my dislike of Nanny Collins, which I was unable to conquer. I called the series *Big Heads and Tiny Bodies*. All the faces were disfigured by hair-sprouting moles and lumps, and eyes on springs, popping out of their ugly faces. The bodies were small and limp, or else there were no bodies, only two thin legs, sprouting straight out of the chin and buckling under the awful weight of the head.

Jo sometimes perfected my grotesques for me, adding horrible hair or skull-and-crossbones earrings. But ugly as they were, they gave me the idea that perhaps, after all, Jo and Aunt June were not the only ones in the family who could draw pictures. By the time we were sent away to school, I drew and painted quite well.

How long did Nanny Collins last? Was it weeks, or months? If the time was miserable for us, then it was also surely miserable for her. And as our parents suggested, she was probably a perfectly nice woman. She just wasn't Vera Sturt, our Nan.

I don't remember enduring a school holiday with Nanny Collins. She never came to the Trusted house in Cornwall. But I don't remember the day she left and Nan came back either, which is odd. We must have longed and longed for that day. And then it got lost in my memory somehow. Perhaps it was that Nan had been so present in our minds while she was away nursing Lilian and Judy that there was some kind of imaginative continuum joining her absence to her reappearance. In she came and our world resumed its former shape, without any awkwardness or fuss or reproach.[1] She was back. That was all that mattered.

And Nan had saved her sister Lilian, a woman

---

[1] In *The Gustav Sonata*, speaking about Beethoven's Piano Sonata No. 26, 'Les Adieux', my protagonist Gustav criticises the optimistic, upbeat tempo of the last movement, which follows the middle section entitled 'L'Absence'. He notes that the return of a loved person, after a period of desertion, sometimes generates strong feelings not of instant happiness, but of anger. I know this to be true, in general, but I think that it was not the case here.

I came to know very well a few years later, when I was taken to stay at Meadows, the house Lilian shared with Judy in Dogmersfield in Hampshire — and where Nan stayed until Sissy died and she inherited Sissy's small cottage, also in Dogmersfield.

This was after the great Casting Away, after we'd been sent to Crofton Grange School and Nan had left us. We'd been promised that she would come back for part of each holiday — to the new house, Frilsham Manor, in Berkshire, which our stepfather, Ivo, had bought. Jane had been made to accept how much we both loved Nan, and to have Nan around during the school holidays no doubt seemed useful to her and Ivo.

What neither of them had bargained for was seeing one of us sent home during the school term. But in my first year at Crofton Grange, I was taken ill with appendicitis, rushed to hospital in Ware to have my appendix taken out, and sent home. We were midway through the summer term.

Jane did her best. I remember that we did some sewing together, confecting a new face for Piggy, whose nose had suffered a terrible burning in front of the nursery fire and was now in shreds. Jane was patient and careful about this. We bought some soft pink fabric in Newbury to match the original stockinet. When the moment came to remove Piggy's eyes, she sent me out of the room and told me to stay out until they were sewn on again in the new face. The operation was a grand success.

Jane was happier now, in a big, comfortable

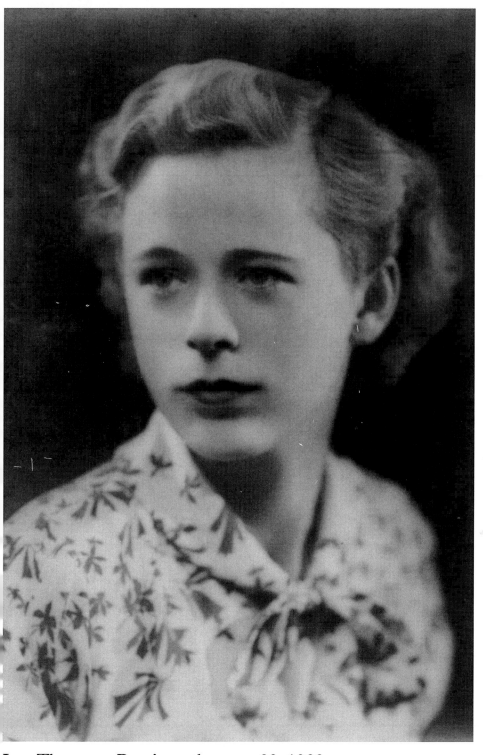

Jane Thomson, Rose's mother, age 20, 1933

Keith Thomson, Rose's father, age 35, 1947

Linkenholt Manor, home of Roland and Mabel Dudley,
Rose's grandparents, *c.*1950

Rose's first birthday picnic, 2 August 1944: baby Rose sitting,
front left

David's Cottage, where Rose saw the birds on the wire

Michael Dudley, Rose's uncle, ready for war, 1940

Nan and Jane outside 22 Sloane Avenue, 1950

Rose and Jo in Wengen with Nan, 1950

Rose near the Meadows canal with Piggy, Mary and Polly, 1954

Timmy Trusted with family Pekinese in Cornwall, c.1950

Jane with Jo and the cousins, Jonathan (left) and Robert (right),
Swanage, 1951

School photo, Crofton Grange, 1953: Rose is second row, second from left

Painting scenery for *The Mysteries of Udolpho*: Jane McKenzie kneeling, left, Elsa Buckley seated, centre, Rose standing, far right

Rose's last school report, defaced by V. M. T.

Signed photo of Poet Laureate John Masefield in his
Oxford study, 1959

Frilsham Manor in the 1960s

The 'ginnery' at Frilsham

Rose being 'finished' at Les Diablerets, Switzerland, 1960

On the balcony at Chardon: Ginny Lathbury (with perm),
second left, Rose next to Carol Reunert, far right

Fondue at the Café de la Poste, Les Diablerets:
left to right: Rose, Jenny Lowe, Pierrette Monod, Carol Reunert

Ski instructor Monsieur Borloz – 'tits to the valley'

Happy at last?: Ivo and Jane Thomson fishing in Ireland, c.1980

Loving Eleanor: Jane with Rose and baby Eleanor, 1972

Trying to love Mother: Rose with Jane, 1992

Smokers' corner: Richard Holmes with Jane at High House,
Norfolk, 1993

Rose with Mawkie at the Lychgate, Linkenholt, 2002

country house, with a man who loved her far more than Keith had ever done, but there was still a limit to how much mothering she was prepared to do. So it was decided I would go and stay with Nan at Meadows.

I was eleven years old, perhaps rather noisy and agitated, feeling everything far too deeply, difficult to tame and calm. I should remember, too, that Jane and Ivo were still in their honeymoon period. They had found a new kind of happiness at Frilsham Manor and they didn't want this to be disturbed. They'd assumed that the children would be safely away until July.

So a suitcase was packed for me and Ivo drove me to Meadows. A camp bed was put up for me in Nan's room. Lilian and Judy welcomed me with a tea of boiled eggs and bread and butter. I was told the eggs came from chickens Lilian kept in a pen at the end of the garden, and that I would be able to help with caring for the birds. And I remember telling Lilian that I knew how to do this because Jo and I and our cousins had done it at Linkenholt, helping Mr Daubeny. So straight away, I was given this lovely task, of feeding the hens each morning and helping to collect the eggs.

Children love tasks — the feeling of being trusted with something important; the joy of doing it, wrong or right. Bossy, perfectionist parents who insist on doing everything them-selves, in case their children make mistakes, are rewarded by having to suffer anxious kids. And the time I spent at Meadows, with its routine of caring for the chickens, was very happy. If I

81

sometimes wondered why my mother had sent me there, when there was now a beautiful new home for me to be in, then Lilian and Judy must surely have wondered about it too. Why did they and not my mother have the burden of caring for me? But both these sisters had about them the same quality of gentleness I so loved in Nan, and they treated me with great kindness.

I remember that the room I shared with Nan at low-lying Meadows had a very small window, and that when I looked out of this each morning, there was almost always a strange blue mist covering everything and a sun like a silver coin in the sky. And then the mist would lift and I would stand at the window and see water at the end of the garden — water with no hint of a ripple on it, sliding by in a slow green drift. And I was told by Lilian that this was a man-made canal, down which boats would still pass and where, if I was very still and quiet at its edge, I might see water snakes.

Nan and I spent a lot of time walking along the banks of the canal. I both wanted to see water snakes and didn't want to see them. Rising up from the muddy bottom of the water were dark brown water weeds, moving and bending in the slow current, and I can remember asking Nan whether these slimy things were 'pretending to be water snakes'.

'Whatever next!' said Nan.

Did we ever see actual snakes? I think we did, but I can't be certain. It always frightened me, in my early life, when I recognised something I thought I knew seeming to undergo troubling alteration so as to resemble something else: a dress standing up on the floor, like a headless person; tears that turned to blood on my pillow; flamingos used as croquet mallets in *Alice in Wonderland*; slimy weeds moving like living reptiles.

And yet you could say that my childhood was defined by the huge, life-changing alteration that I longed to bring about. I didn't want Jane to be my mother; I wanted Nan to be my mother.

I used to fantasise that there would be some colossal Moment of Revelation (over elevenses in the nursery, perhaps — the setting for the utterance of so much shock news) when Vera Sturt would be revealed as my true parent and Jane would be sent away — back to do her shopping in Liberty's, with its glass cabinet in a thousand pieces on the floor; back into the darkness of the nightclubs where she loved to dance.

But it never happened.

Carolyn Slaughter was right to designate Nan as my angel, as the person who saved my sanity — and probably that of my only child, my daughter Eleanor, who, thanks to the love I'd been given by Nan, was able to become the recipient of the mother-love in me and in turn show deep and unwavering affection towards her own two children.

Angels in the Bible appear and disappear in flaming glory, in blinding light. They announce the most breathtaking events. But Nan was never able to appear as a winged messenger, telling me what I wanted to hear. She was just an ordinary woman, a little lonely, a little disappointed by life, a person who loved flowers and knitting and funicular trains and classic serials on the radio. She'd also loved Peter Taylor, her first charge, and, by some miracle, she discovered in her heart a willingness to love Jo and me.

# The English Room

Crofton Grange School was housed in a large mansion near the small village of Braughing (pronounced Braffing), in Hertfordshire. The facade of the building was grand, with 'Tudor remnants' still showing here and there among its heavy restoration, which dated from the 1830s. Neither the Tudors nor the Victorians had been able to heat the house properly, and the builders who had converted it into a school in the 1940s had made only half-hearted attempts to warm up a few of the ground-floor rooms with heavy iron radiators. My most afflicting memory of Crofton Grange is of the eternal cold we all endured.

There was a 'school ghost', who went by the Dickensian name of Miss Mellish, a woman who had reputedly been murdered on the grand Tudor staircase. I suppose she was the ultimate Tudor remnant, and we all longed to terrify ourselves by catching sight of her. My friend Elsa Buckley has always claimed that she *did* see Miss Mellish, that the ghost 'came floating up the stairs, in purple'. Of course, it *had* to be purple, a colour perfectly aligned with the vivid imaginations of teenage girls, and I don't remember Elsa being frightened, just rather privileged to have been the one to see Miss M.

Around the front of the house was a ha-ha, designed to keep animals from straying onto the lawns, but there were no animals any more; the ha-ha was there now, it seemed, only to keep us *in*. Beyond the ha-ha was a park, leading on one side to some beautiful beechwoods, known as the Mentley Woods, where we were allowed to walk at weekends. We were not free, even in the woods; we were prisoners of the school. Trespass beyond the gates and you were expelled. Yet there was an illusion of freedom, for what this park became was a vast green amphitheatre for conversation.

Walking there in our 'outdoor shoes', away from the gaze of the teachers and the prefects, in little huddles of two or three, we dissected our teenage hearts. Our favourite places to perch were the fallen trees that were strewn across the park like wrecked ships. Sucking on grasses in the summer, or eating raw elderberries to try to assuage our perpetual hunger, we exchanged anxieties and dreams.

What did upper-middle-class girls — in such a place, in rural England in the 1950s — actually talk about? Did we have anything interesting to say to each other? We were polite, innocent children, who knew hardly anything about the world. The word 'politics' had almost no meaning for us. And the nearest we got to rebellion was to play Tommy Steele's 'Singing the Blues' on the school gramophone. We lived in a pre-Elvis world.

Later, after that voice from some measureless cavern of desire had touched us, we'd talk about boys we'd met in the holidays, from whom we constantly hoped for cards and letters. But in my first years at Crofton Grange, what we talked about most was our exile — from our homes, from 'proper' food, from warmth, from our distracted parents (or, in my case, from Nan) and from a past that appeared suddenly nurturing and benign. This shared exile confected a bond between us and, on the whole, made us kind to each other.

There was some bullying in the school. I remember that we sometimes gave the (very few) fat girls a miserable time. A girl with an irritating adenoidal voice was parodied and shunned — all the more cruelly because her parents were Christian Scientists, who refused all medical intervention for their daughter. We occasionally settled quarrels by bashing each other with lacrosse sticks or stealing each other's sweets, but mainly we wanted to make friends and discover ways to make bearable what, at its core, was an unbearable situation for us all.

We were never made to suffer physical beatings. The worst punishments at Crofton Grange all involved missing some longed-for treat: the Saturday-night play put on by each class in turn, the Hallowe'en supper, the Guy Fawkes Night firework display. But for the generation of boys sent away to school in the 1950s in Britain, now men in their sixties and seventies, corporal punishment was a hideous part of day-to-day life. This descended down the generations, with small boys who had been caned for minor rule infringements growing up to become prefects who in their turn had beating rights.

How did the lads survive, in the face of this

constant terror? First-hand accounts given to me by friends and relations of this age group all recall feelings of perpetual dread, lasting years. But in A. A. Milne's 1939 autobiography, *It's Too Late Now*, he wrote: 'I was happy at school [Westminster, where he, too, was beaten] only because I had to be at school and must therefore get what happiness I could out of it.' So I suppose this was what all the boys had to do — get what happiness they could — and I think, after the first bad bout of homesickness, most of us at Crofton Grange made some similar sort of resolution.

Yet for the first couple of years, we never stopped longing for time to pass, to release us back into our families — or what remained of them. At the start of every term, we drew what we called a 'term worm' at the back of our prep books. The worm was divided up into segments — one for each day — and the days were coloured in the moment they'd passed. Sometimes, down the length of the worm, there lurked some anticipated happiness — a parents' day celebration, a half-term weekend — and I remember that I coloured these in before I got to them, partly to make them stand out, but also knowing already that — such is the teasing nature of time — they would be over almost before they had begun.

★ ★ ★

Our Crofton day started at five past seven, when the matron and the two under-matrons woke us

88

by sticking thermometers into our mouths. These thermometers were housed in little glass tumblers of TCP, and the smell of this medication can still make me gag. Round the dormitories the matrons marched, dressed in white overalls and little starched head-dresses, the tiaras of the school-medics' world. They stuck the thermometers under our tongues, hurried on to another dorm, then marched back in, snatching the thermometers out again, reading them with practised, laser eyes and passing on to the next bed.

There were almost one hundred girls at Crofton Grange and about thirty thermometers, so each thermometer went from TCP to mouth and back again three times every morning. More than the dread of the TCP, I used to fear the taste of another girl's mouth, stale from sleep, tainted by last night's supper of macaroni cheese — or worse, by some vomiting that had occurred during the night.

Now and again, I tried to cheat the thermometer reading by heating it on my body. In my first year, I'd lost the art of falling asleep at bed-time — that sweet descent which had seemed so easy when I shared a room with Nan — so I began most days feeling tired, sometimes so deeply exhausted that I longed to succumb to illness and be sent to the san, which was heated with a gas fire and where you were allowed to listen to *Housewives' Choice* on an old Roberts wireless.

The deception with the thermometer seldom worked, because there wasn't enough time for the temperature to rise before the tiara brigade returned. So my bedding would be pulled back and I'd stagger around in search of underpants, vest and socks, often feeling almost insane from lack of sleep. Children's bodies need a lot of deep rest and mine was often so starved of it that I had bouts of hallucination.

We had exactly half an hour to wash and dress — in yesterday's underwear, in the day-before-yesterday's underwear, in three- or four-day old underwear — because nothing was laundered more than once a week. Hair-washing — done in a basin — was a rationed activity and there were no showers, only ancient baths of stained enamel, with a line marking the permitted height of the water, to which we had access twice a week. I think we all stank like polecats.

After tugging on our grimy clothes, we lined up and went down the back stairs to the hall, where we waited for the headmistress, Mrs Baines, the head girl and the prefects to descend the main staircase (up which Miss Mellish's ghost had once floated for Elsa) and to take their places in the dining room before we filed in for breakfast.

The kitchen staff at Crofton Grange were Italian. They did their best, I guess, with cheap ingredients and, until 1956, post-war rationing, but hunger gnawed at us all, right through our school years. Ninety-nine per cent of us were stick thin. We were expected to play lacrosse or tennis every afternoon on a very low-calorie diet. Supper was sometimes nothing more than bread and cheese and water. Tea was bread and jam. If some girls put on flesh, it was no doubt because of this bread-choked diet.

The best meal was breakfast, for which the Italians often made a delicious kind of hash out of bacon and onion that we called bacon pudding, and sometimes there were sausages — one each — served with Italian tinned tomatoes. If your parents had agreed to pay extra, you were allowed an orange at breakfast, but Jane had told me and Jo that she was 'paying quite enough, thank you very much', so we never got the oranges, and it's interesting to observe that I still think of an orange as some kind of precious fruit. To start my day, as I often do now, with freshly squeezed orange juice still strikes me as a secret luxury.

The bacon pudding was washed down with weak coffee, drunk out of mottled green plastic cups. When it was your turn to sit at Mrs Baines's table, she would encourage you to 'make a lifelong habit of avoiding sugar in coffee'. No doubt she wanted to save on rations and on catering funds, but we all took her seriously and tried to please her because she was the headmistress, and so lingering and effective was this command, I have never been able to bear the taste of sugared coffee, down the whole pathway of my life since that time.

After breakfast, we began lessons. The classrooms were designated not by class, but by subject. The history room was the only one with a heater, put in there, we supposed, because the history teacher, Miss Vermidge, was best friends with Mrs Baines. The Latin room and the art room were housed in wooden huts. Our favourite room, despite the cold, was the English room.

In winter, for most lessons, I wore blue-and-pink fingerless gloves, knitted by Nan, thus saving myself from the chilblains from which many girls suffered. How we were able to concentrate in these freezing little spaces, I can't quite recall. A deep longing for spring, for the sight of a daisy pushing up on the slopes of the ha-ha, was acute in all of us all through the winter term.

The teachers' bedrooms were warmed by gas fires, but how did they survive the glacial classrooms? A defining image of Crofton Grange, for me, was the sight of our English teacher, Miss Ida Robinson — whom I came to know and admire, with something akin to love — reciting the poems of Keats wearing a ratty fur coat, from which she was seldom parted. She tucks the collar of the coat round her thin neck as she begins:

Season of mists and mellow fruitfulness,
Close bosom-friend of the maturing sun,
Conspiring with him how to load and bless
With fruit the vines that round the thatch-
    eaves run . . .

In my second year, Miss Robinson asked me to paint an 'illustrated' version of 'To Autumn' to go up on the English room wall. On stiff, expensive white paper, I made a complex border for the poem, featuring hazel twigs, poppies, standing sheaves, 'mossed cottage trees', bees, gnats, robins and swallows. When this was done, the moment to copy in the poem arrived.

I selected a calligraphy pen and black ink. I was proud of how good my handwriting could be, when I paid attention. (My father had exquisite writing, and I suppose I tried to copy this.)

Then I spoilt the whole thing with a spelling mistake in the first line. I can't read or hear this poem without remembering the terrible blunder, which couldn't be rectified: 'Season of mists and mellow *fruitulness*'. I felt covered with shame.

Yet my love of Keats's work wasn't affected by this. When ill in bed recently, I spent two solid days reading the 2001 Folio edition of *The Complete Poems* and loved every moment of them. Simon Brett's engravings for this collection are also very fine, leading you seductively forward from one poem to the next.

Of all the teachers at Crofton Grange, Miss Robinson was the only true intellectual. Her background was her 'beloved Oxford'. She was a close friend of the Poet Laureate, John Masefield. She had been engaged to a fellow student at Oxford, who had died in the war before they could be married — or so went the narrative we told each other about her. But was this true? I can't say for sure. I think we may just have wanted to believe that a woman as passionate about literature as Ida Robinson had had some physical passion in her youth. We already understood that for many women of her generation, love had passed them by altogether. Apart from Mrs Baines, who was a widow, none of the teachers at Crofton Grange had ever been married.

We called Miss Robinson 'Robbie', when out of her hearing. Robbie's deep feeling for Shakespeare's language, which she understood as well as 'the cat sat on the mat', untangled the words and found the rhythms for us so effortlessly that we were quickly led to precocious epiphanies of understanding.

I remember that we began *Romeo and Juliet* in my first term, when I was just eleven. I've never forgotten my encounter with this play. Over the many productions of *Romeo and Juliet* that I've seen throughout my life, it's still Robbie's voice that I sometimes hear, reciting while gazing out of the English room window at the snow falling on the park. This speech is spoken by Romeo at dawn, after the secretly married lovers have spent the night together and can't endure the idea that morning will part them:

Let me be ta'en, let me be put to death;
I am content, so thou wilt have it so.
I'll say yon grey is not the morning's eye,
'Tis but the pale reflex of Cynthia's brow;
Nor that is not the lark, whose notes do beat
The vaulty heaven so high above our heads:
I have more care to stay than will to go:
Come death and welcome! Juliet wills it so.

'Now unpack it for me,' says Robbie. 'What is 'yon grey'? 'What does 'reflex' mean here? Who is Cynthia?' And I suppose, at the beginning, we looked completely blank and Robbie would have had to answer all her own questions. But here's the thing with Shakespeare's language, if it's well taught: understanding becomes fertile, begets other small moments of revelation, and these lead on and on and multiply until what at first seemed as perplexing as a maths equation ends by unfurling before your eyes an exquisite solution.

Robbie had a thin, sorrowful face — as if, somewhere in her life, she'd seen human agonies she couldn't forget. And some of the time, she was severe with us, slapping down the heavy dictionary on our desks when we got a word wrong and turning her back on us — shoulders hunched with fury inside the fur coat — till we'd looked it up and got it right. But when we did well, when we could tell her that Cynthia was not only the moon (with its 'pale reflex' or reflection), but also another name for the goddess Diana, from Mount Cynthus, where she was born, Robbie's face would be transfigured by an extraordinary smile, revealing protruding, untutored teeth.

Robbie was the greatest fount of consolation at Crofton Grange. Not only did she manage to make Shakespeare thrilling for us and give us our first sip of Keats's melancholy, but by doing this — by treating us as 'clever' children — she cemented friendships within our small group. Probably she behaved just the same with other classes (Jo had great respect for her, too), but we chose to believe that she favoured us, Form 2A, and we set aside our homesickness in our efforts to please her.

Jane McKenzie, Elsa Buckley, Julie Phillpotts, Heather Gray, Jane Stern, Marilyn Gillespie, Clare Wainwright, Alison Fairfax-Lucy, Elizabeth Blackadder, Gillian Shepherd, Dallas Hill, Elizabeth Beddington, Deborah Walker and Rosie Thomson . . . we thought of ourselves as Robbie's crew. We didn't mind our forced shackling to the *Oxford English Dictionary*. When we'd found the word she'd asked for, we competed to dash for the blackboard to obey her command: 'Write it down! Write it down!' And for prep (not 'homework', for our homes were far off), she began early asking us to make up stories. 'The imagination,' she told us, 'allows the human mind to escape from the mundane. People with no imagination lead dull lives.'

As a counterbalance to *Romeo and Juliet* and Keats's odes, we were reading John Masefield: *The Midnight Folk* and *Lost Endeavour*. The stories I wrote for Robbie at this time were heavily influenced by the adventures of Masefield's characters, mainly boys, who cross dangerous seas — those seas to which Masefield lost his heart as a young midshipman in the navy — in search of treasure and who find magic potions to make them invisible. The idea of escape from the limits of their world is at the heart of these books, and escape was much on my mind. I longed to disappear and reappear, not beside Masefield's 'lonely sea and the sky', but on the banks of the canal where the water snakes and the slithery weeds lived in terrifying confusion at the end of the Meadows garden, to find Nan at my side.

The moment where Master Kay, in *The Midnight Folk*, finds the 'Invisible Mixture' stayed with me for a long time. Here, invisibility isn't the dangerous, addictive state Tolkien contrives so grippingly in *Lord of the Rings*, but rather a wonderful lark, told wryly. Both author and boy are fascinated by what's happening and yet are also on the verge of laughing at it.

[Kay] had some old sugar lumps put away under the carpet. He took out one of these and carefully opened the bottle. The mixture had a warm, rich smell, like the smell of green bracken on a very hot day. 'I must be very careful of this,' he thought. He dropped three drops on to a lump, popped it in his mouth and re-stoppered the phial. A glow went through him, as though he were sucking the loveliest peppermint ever made. He hid the phial in a mouse-hole in the skirting board behind the valance and then stood up. He felt a pepperminty feeling go tingling along his toes, and lo, he looked at his toes and could not see them, nor his legs, nor his pyjamas, and though he looked at himself in the glass, he was not there: he was invisible. 'I say, what fun,' he said.[1]

An idea that came early to us — or perhaps was suggested by Robbie — was to spend some

---

[1] My copy of the book, a first edition, is dedicated 'For Rosemary, on her birthday, from John Masefield'.

of the art class time making pictures of scenes from Masefield's books. The art teacher, Miss Felicity Ashbee, a splendidly handsome bohemian woman, with the face of a gypsy and fine, expressive hands, had to be consulted, but she gave her blessing to this and so we began on a series of pictures of pirates and gamekeepers, desert islands, raging seas, three-masted clippers, witches and wise owls.

We worked in poster paints on coarse sugar paper. The idea of the 'series' gave a satisfying professional edge to our labours and bonded us further. We were the 'John Masefield Class'. Elsa's pictures were the best, but mine weren't too bad and everybody worked hard at this enterprise.[1] Robbie was so delighted with the end result that she hung them all round the English room walls (my Keats blunder having mercifully disappeared), and they stayed there a long time. She also wrote to John Masefield asking him if would like to see them, and this letter led, eventually, to a visit to Oxford and an encounter with the great man.

I can't remember when this took place, or how many of us were there, in his house in Oxford. I

---

[1] Elsa — under the name Elsa Taylor — is now a very successful professional artist, who has had one-woman shows in Burford, Sherborne, Truro and London. My close friendship with her still brings me amusement and joy. Two of her wonderful pictures hang in my hall, and I have just bought a third. Some of her work can be viewed at www.elsataylor.co.uk.

know the party included Jane McKenzie and Elsa. What I can recall is that the elderly Masefield was extremely kind to us. While his daughter, Judith, brought in a wonderful spread of tea and cakes, I confided to the elderly Laureate that I wanted 'to follow him' and become a writer. What he said to me in reply is lost in the mist of time. Perhaps, like Master Kay, when confronted by something surprising, he just smiled and said, 'I say, what fun!'

Recently, I've discovered, in a forgotten drawer, a small cache of letters and cards from Masefield, virtually unfaded by time. These reveal that I tried to keep in contact with him by sending him not stories (in which I probably had no confidence and didn't want to embarrass either myself or him by asking him to read them) but flower pictures. In one of the letters, from his house, Burcote Brook, near Abingdon, he writes to thank me for 'these beautiful Columbines and for writing your welcome kind greetings to me in that exquisite script of yours. So many grateful thanks to you. I ought to blush to be writing my thanks to you in a hand like this; but a lot of these old fellows are really past blushing. I think with gladness of your kind young friends and shall ever bless you all and wish you every happiness and delight. I thank you all and shall put your Columbines on my ink stand (made of my old ship). Gratefully yours, John Masefield.'

Was ever an elderly writer more kind and courteous to a group of schoolgirl fans?

★   ★   ★

One inescapable feature of boarding school is all the 'dead time' that blights each and every day: the time between lunch and afternoon games; the gap between the end of lessons at five o'clock and supper at seven; the peculiar, exhausted hours between supper and bed.

Certain extramural activities were arranged for us. Every term, we were compelled to knit a 'charity garment' for orphaned babies. We had to provide our own patterns and our own needles and wool, and if your garment was so badly made that it couldn't be passed on to the orphans' charity, you were punished by missing the last-night supper, where cider cup was served.

Jane McKenzie was tragically bad at knitting, and her charity garments — pocked moonscapes of holes and dropped stitches — had to be unpicked and rescued term after term by her friends. Jo and I, who had been taught to knit by Nan, had no difficulty with this task. I remember that I found knitting consoling in its slow, repetitive unfolding. And after a few terms, I began making designs on graph paper for knitted motifs — ladybirds, flowers and birds — to be incorporated into my garments. I remember liking the idea that some little orphan girl or boy would be dressed in a matinee jacket decorated with wild things.

The knitting hour came after lunch, while we digested the grey mince and watery cabbage, the sponge cake and custard that had to sustain us till supper time. We sat around in the big school drawing room, where we sang evening prayers and where the vicar of Braughing church sometimes came to talk to us about God, which he liked to emphasise as 'the Word made Flesh'. The room smelled of mothballs and beeswax polish, but we were so crowded together in the knitting hour that after we'd all been there for half an hour, it smelled of flesh — of unwashed armpits, dirty hair and menstrual blood.

In the cold hour between the end of lessons and supper, we congregated in the wooden prep hall. This was when I raced through my work and started drawing what became known as 'Rosie's beauty contests', passing my rough book, with crayoned pictures of girls' heads, sporting different colouring and hairstyles, surreptitiously from desk to desk till it came back to me with the results, which would arrive with comments something like these: from Elsa, 'Number three is a clear winner. Super hair!' From Heather, 'I love number one. Wish I was blonde.' From Julie, 'Number nine reminds me of me — but better.' From our only French girl, Sabine, 'J'aime ta dixième. Son nez retroussé surtout. C'est elle qui gagne.'

Something shocking and extraordinary was related to us by Sabine when she was fourteen: she wasn't a virgin any more, as the rest of us were; she had made love with her father. She told us this very calmly, explaining that her father believed that 'The first lover of a woman must take great care of her and I can only reassure myself that this will happen by taking care of her myself.' Looking back, I can't remember any signs that Sabine was traumatised by this. She spoke about it in a contented, almost boastful way. Had it, in fact, happened, or was it some teenage illusion of hers? If it had happened, then perhaps, in later life, she came to suffer for it and even see her life destroyed by it. Or perhaps not. She was a wide-faced, almost pretty girl, with a gentle temperament and eyes of piercing blue. I have often wondered what became of her.

Despite knitting and prep and beauty contests, time still dragged. In my third year, aged thirteen, my friend Heather Gray and I decided our lives would be much more interesting if we were in love. There were no men to fall in love with — only the tennis coach, Ray, who couldn't say his r's properly and so was unkindly known as 'Way'. (Naturally, he called me 'Wosie'.) We settled on the mannish but striking geography teacher, Miss Jean Howard.

It was summer. We stole a red rose from one of the garden borders and scattered the petals in front of her cottage. We approached her after one of her lessons and told her we *adored* geography and wanted her to supervise extra work. We offered to do more drawings of artesian wells and Maori warriors.

What were we hoping for? Deep attention, I think: something that told us Jean Howard thought we were special. All children sent away from home, as we had been, long to be singled out by their teachers and others in positions of authority. I know that Heather and I also fantasised what it would be like to be kissed by her. In fact, we never made that kind of

102

approach, never indulged in any physical touching of Miss Howard. But the more we *told* ourselves we were in love, the more real and absorbing this fantasy seemed to be.[1]

★ ★ ★

In the studies, the only heated rooms in the main house, two daily newspapers were laid out for us, *The Times* and the *Daily Telegraph*. We were expected to use some of our free time to read these and learn about the world. Once a week, at Saturday assembly, our knowledge was tested. This test was known as current events, and such was the paper shortage in the 1950s, that we wrote our answers on the backs of old envelopes extracted from Mrs Baines's waste-paper basket.

Perhaps it was the fact that we were in a rural prison, so that the great happenings of the post-war world seemed so very distant from us, but I remember that we always found this test irksome, mainly did badly at it because we

---

[1] Years later, I wrote a short story, 'Extra Geography', published in my collection *The American Lover*, in which two sporty girls, Minna and Flic, experience extreme boredom at school and decide to fall in love with the next person they see. The next person they see is the female geography teacher, a New Zealander called Rosalind Delavigne. Minna and Flic are much more determined than we were to be kissed by Rosalind, and as a result of this, the story moves towards a tragic denouement.

hadn't spent enough time reading *The Times* and the *Daily Telegraph*, and longed for it to be over.

Elsa has found a passage in a diary she kept in 1956, at the time of the Suez Crisis, where she reveals Robbie saying: 'The only way we can help is to trust in God and He alone will help us.' We know now what a dark moment this was for the Western world, and no doubt we tried to answer questions about it on our torn envelopes during current events, but at age thirteen, despite Robbie's intimations of apocalypse, the elements that had brought the crisis about somehow floated free of our attention. We knew that Britain and France, the old, arrogant colonial powers, were now trembling before a dark-browed 'villain' called Colonel Nasser, but who exactly was he, and even if we understood properly who he was, what could we do about it?

Did we talk about Suez amongst ourselves? I can't remember. There was no debating society at Crofton Grange, no nurturing of political awareness, so I think we probably said almost nothing to each other about a world in crisis, but just carried on with our minuscule, girlie lives. Round come the thermometers dunked in TCP, Tuesdays dawn and serve up the wonderful bacon pudding, our charity garments begin to take shape, tea is bread and jam again, a cold wind sighs over the lacrosse field, one of Mrs Baines's Norfolk terriers shits on the kitchen step, the Italian cooks scream at each other, Robbie recites *Hamlet*, Heather and I wait outside the vegetable garden for a sighting of Miss Howard, I lie in the dark, not sleeping . . .

★　★　★

During these vacant, exhausting nights, I thought often about my lost father and, as a kind of homage to him, decided to begin writing plays.

The school acknowledged that drama coaching might be important for the developing mind. Under the careful eye of Miss Jill Bostock, the young drama teacher, our form had already embarked on a herculean production of an adaptation of Ann Radcliffe's *The Mysteries of Udolpho*. The most arduous task for this production was the painting of the scenery. But unspoken in us, I think, was a yearning for the arduous, to take our minds off the home lives we couldn't quite forget. Elsa agrees with me about this. Making things challenging for ourselves was a fundamental aim of our Crofton lives.

We'd resolved that 'the whole three walls of the stage', normally draped with faded red curtains, against which a few token props were installed, had to be completely covered by the stone walls of the castle. To do this, Miss Ashbee agreed to order in swathes of canvas and supporting batons. We laid the canvas out on the grass in front of the art room and, kneeling — or even lying down — in our brown overalls, gradually painted in a colossal acreage of gothic stonework, mullion windows, crumbling pillars and colonies of bats.

It was a work of weeks and weeks. I think we spent more time creating the castle than we did rehearsing the play, but when the curtain finally went up on its one night of existence, the whole school broke into astonished applause. No matter if the acting was a bit mediocre, if Jane McKenzie, as the heroine Emily, was a touch wooden, if Heather, as the dashing Valancourt, was a bit too beefy for her velvet breeches, if my death as Emily's father was stagey; the *set* was brilliant. And for this, our *Udolpho* won the end-of-term drama cup. I remember that we all trooped up to receive it, and no actor climbing the scintillating stage to receive her Oscar has ever felt more proud.

CROFTON GRANGE.

2nd November, 1957

Piano Solos

Sonata in G minor (first movement)—*Beethoven*
E. von Petersdorff
Prelude in C sharp minor—*Rachmaninoff* .......... C. Hulton

Song

The Song of the Music Makers—*Martin Shaw*

THE MYSTERIES OF UDOLPHO
by Mrs. Radcliffe

Scene: The Castle Udolpho.

Emily ............................................................. J. McKenzie
Madame Montoni ...................................... J. Stern
Signor Montoni ....................................... R. Thomson
Annette ................................................... J. Phillpotts
Caterina ...................................................... D. Hill
Count Morano ........................................ C. Wainwright
Count Verezzi .......................................... E. Blackadder
Signora Laurentini .................................. M. Gillespie
Count Valancourt ..................................... H. Gray
Count du Pont .......................................... E. Buckley
Count Bartolini ........................................ D. Walker

It was a short step, then, from here to the idea that I might *write* a play we could perform.

My first effort was about two pampered girls who decide to see the world by offering themselves as cleaners to rich Italians, Americans and vodka-quaffing Russians. The whole idea was preposterous and the play deserved the mediocre reception that it got. It was a disappointment to me, of course, but I thought of Keith and all his disappointments, and pressed on.

I followed this first play with a work titled *Always a Clown*, thus ushering in another epic period of scene-painting, to create a circus arena. This, coupled with a rather moving performance from Jane Stern as the titular clown, and some stirring music (Sibelius's symphonic poem *Finlandia*) to accompany his/her dream of thwarted love, gave a sentimental story some much-needed ballast. At least it expressed its distance from the short mysteries and drawing-room comedies that were the normal fare of form plays. And once again, the difficulty of the whole project inspired us as a group and brought us together. Another good thing happened, all the more miraculous for being unexpected: on the morning of the play, a telegram arrived from Keith, saying, 'Congratulations on your first first night. Love, Dad.'

I kept this for a long time, but eventually it got thrown out, along with all my teenage letters and notebooks. I would give quite a lot to have some of these bits of my juvenile archive back. I envy Elsa her diary. But ninety per cent of all my records are gone and that's that. What I can remember is that after *Always a Clown*, I was no longer unhappy at Crofton Grange. In fact, I was enthralled by all the work that could be done there. And — ironic though this may sound — when the longed-for holidays came round, I discovered in myself a peculiar unease that at first I couldn't identify. Then, one afternoon, in my comfortable room at Frilsham Manor, I realised with something like shock that I was bored. I wanted to be back at school, painting scenery, learning Shakespeare, singing in the choir, playing the piano — and writing.

★ ★ ★

Throughout my professional writing life, which has now lasted forty years, I've very often been asked: 'How did you come to be a writer?' Are writers 'born'? people wonder. Or do we struggle extremely hard to rebirth ourselves in this new guise? And if so, when and how is this rebirthing achieved?

The origins of our writing selves are all different. Some writers, like my old friend and mentor Angus Wilson, who didn't 'discover' himself as a novelist until he was forty, come to it late, after they've embarked on other careers. The great Penelope Fitzgerald 'knew' she was a writer when an undergraduate at Oxford, but wasn't able — because of family commitments and the need to earn regular money — to find the time to write novels until she was sixty.

For me, there are various answers, or perhaps what I should call 'a list of ingredients' present in the true answer. These ingredients go more or less like this:

- My father was a writer. For all Dad's lack of real success, I grew up with the idea that a writer was an honourable thing to become.

- My mother had no job or profession whatso-ever. I knew I didn't want to copy her life.
- My sister was destined to be an artist. I wanted to be destined to be *something*.
- I quickly found that trying to evoke alternative worlds in stories or plays was an efficient antidote to homesickness and self-pity.
- Through all the work done in the English room at Crofton Grange with Ida Robinson, I began to understand that great literature shed light on the human condition in a way that nothing else could. (No, not even art or music — or not for me, anyway.) So why not try to contribute, in however small a way, to that necessary illumination?

But there is also one memorable moment, a summertime epiphany, when I was thirteen or fourteen, which confirmed in me the certainty that writing was the *only* thing I wanted to do, and that my life would be somehow half lived — or what Martin Amis has memorably called 'thin' — if I couldn't establish this at the centre of my world.

It was a summer afternoon at Crofton. I'd been playing tennis after tea. The sun was just beginning a showy descent above the hayfield that separated the tennis courts from the garden. My tennis partners had wandered away and I found myself alone, wearing shorts and a white Aertex shirt, carrying my tennis racquet (in its wooden press, of course), on the path through the hay, which had just been cut.

I stopped walking and stood still on the path.

The perfume of the hay, the heat of my body after the tennis game, the sky the colour of coral, the silence surrounding me — all combined to fill me, suddenly, with a profound feeling of wonder, a fleeting sense of the marvellous, which, in its intensity, was almost a visionary experience.

I told myself that if I continued standing still, this moment would last and might even change me in some way that I couldn't quite foresee. But I stood there so long that the sun almost disappeared and the field became full of shadows. And with the dusk came a feeling of desolation. The desolation was simply a mundane recognition of the fleeting nature of everything, which even teenagers (or perhaps *especially* teenagers) understand. A moment of happiness as intense as this slips quickly away with the turning of the earth. So I asked myself, there in the hayfield, with the sweat of the tennis game drying down my back and making me shiver: was there any way in which the experiences of my life, like this one, could be captured and locked away, not just in capricious, gradually fading memory, but in some more concrete form?

I walked back to the school with the answer to my question. It *could* be captured. I would write a *story* about the hayfield. It wouldn't be a mundane account of what had happened to me; it would be transfigured by becoming fiction. It wouldn't be re-experienced as sentimental nostalgia, but experienced *afresh*. In this way it could become new again — that was the revelation. As the author of the story, I wouldn't tamely and passively submit to it; I would assert my divinity over it.

I can't remember whether I told any of my friends about this. Writers tend to keep precious revelations and sudden, blinding ideas to themselves, aware, as D.H. Lawrence pointed out in his 1922 *Essays*, that the telling of them can diminish them and make them unusable as ideas for stories. Lawrence went so far as to say that he couldn't tell anybody he loved them, because the saying of the words 'I love you' immediately negated them. I wouldn't agree with him here; expressing what one *thinks* one feels can sometimes bring it, blinking, into the bright realm of certainty. However, I have always recognised that knowledge is a powerful thing, and knowing when to keep it secret is an art which every serious writer needs to perfect.

# Teen Music

Now I have to go back to Sir Ivo Thomson and the house he bought for us after his marriage to my mother: the very beautiful Frilsham Manor, near Newbury in Berkshire.

Ivo had made enough money out of the sales of his shares in the *Yorkshire Evening Press* to stop work in his fifties and settle into the life of a country squire. A tributary of the Pang river ran through the garden at Frilsham Manor, which he and Jane stocked with trout so that they could go fishing whenever the mood took them. It took them quite often, because they had nothing much else to do. And dry-fly fishing, I now understand, was a kind of life's bond for them, the thing they both loved and at which — after taking lessons — they became quite skilled. All their favourite holidays were spent on the great trout rivers of the British Isles, the Kennet, the Test, the Avon, the Wye, the Tweed and the Usk.

The garden at Frilsham was large and well set out, with soft lawns, beautiful river borders, an orchard and a walled potager, which provided vegetables and herbs for the kitchen all year round. Jane sometimes worked there, doing what she called 'little bits', and Ivo memorably walked up and down the orchard, pushing a noisy rotor mower, turning a bright shade of pink all over his body, which amused us children and worried Jane. But the garden was mainly looked after by a man called Jim Butler, a quiet, patient person who always moved with a slow step, as if anxious not to disturb any bird, plant or flower, and who understood deep in his bones how to care for the soil.

Ivo, our father's first cousin, was now the anchor of a newly constructed family. Jo and I acquired Mark (Mawkie) and Carol Thomson as our step-siblings. Jane acquired them as her stepchildren and was never entirely at ease with either of them. Mawkie was two years older than me — twelve when the Frilsham family came together — and Carol was seventeen or eighteen and on the verge of leaving home to start her adult life.

Jo and I were both struck dumb by Carol. She was exceptionally beautiful, in a blonde, Grace Kelly-ish way. Her skin was peachy. Her hair — unlike ours — seemed always obedient to her will. It was difficult to think of this person as our sister. Perhaps some memory of her mother, Tweets, emerging from her dress on the nursery floor always clung to Carol, making us slightly afraid of her. Her beauty certainly ensured that she had a legion of devoted lovers in her twenties — thus increasing the awe we felt for her. I remember that one or two of these were brought down to Frilsham and crept into Carol's room after the parents had gone to bed and put in their ear plugs. She eventually married Commander Mike Parker, an equerry to Prince Philip. Carol and Mike had one daughter, Kate. The marriage was good, I think, for as long as it lasted, but Carol's life was destined to be unbearably short. She died of cancer in her early forties. I was never able to have with her any of those 'looking back' conversations that I've often had (and still have) with Mawkie. What she thought of me and Jo I never really found out. The only thing I remember her saying to me, when I was dressed for a party in a pretty black-and-white dress Jane had bought for me in London, and wearing a tiny touch of my first lipstick (Roman Pink, by Max Factor), was that I looked like a doll.

Mawkie was a lovable, handsome boy with a thatch of red hair, an infectious laugh and a mild penchant for rebellion against Ivo and Jane and authority in general. He and I loved rowing up and down the river in a tiny wooden boat, but we were never allowed to go on the lowest stretch of it, in case we toppled over the little weir that ran beside an old mill house at the end of the garden and broke the boat — and our necks — on the concrete channel that carried the water away in a fast current. But I can remember how the weir called to us. As you got nearer to it, you could feel the flow of the water speed up and the boat begin its fatal glide towards the precipice. Then you would have to row as hard as you could, one oar each, to save yourself from catastrophe. It was the kind of game, the kind of risk that teenagers adore, something that has real danger in it and which is certain to bring about parental mayhem. Jo — wisely perhaps — stayed out of these boating escapades, but Mawkie and I repeated them as often as we dared. Sometimes, Ivo would come rushing along the riverbank, signalling wildly to us, like a stationmaster trying to slow down a runaway train with a red flag. But as far as I can recall, we just waved to him and rowed calmly on, giggling no doubt, pulling slowly towards the weir and then suddenly away from it.

★   ★   ★

Ivo could get angry with us, but in the main, we were lucky to have this sane and affectionate man as our substitute father. This branch of the Thomson family were Yorkshiremen (descended from our great-grandfather, William Thomson, Archbishop of York from 1862 until his death in 1890), and there was always something of the Yorkshire character in Ivo — amused, stubborn, outspoken and kind.

After the breaking apart of the three couples (the two Thomson families and the Whitmee family) in London and the distress of all the children, Ivo understood that it was he who had to try to repair some of the damage. He made leaving our home in London bearable by buying a spacious and pretty house in one of those chalky Berkshire valleys that still tug at my heart. He provided for Jane the kind of lifestyle she aspired to and which my father had never been able to afford.

Was my mother happy?

What I think happened when she married Ivo was that she felt a profound gratitude to him for rescuing her from heartbreak — for rescuing us all — and that she tried as hard as she could to

115

be happy. I recall that she also tried to be kinder to me and Jo, but this attempt would very often falter.

One of these falterings occurred on my thirteenth birthday, 2 August 1956. As my birthday treat, Ivo drove us in the Bentley to Swanage beach. Jane had prepared a picnic lunch of cold roast chicken, mayonnaise and hard-boiled eggs. A birthday cake waited in a tin.

The day began well, with the sun shining on the water and Jane and Ivo drinking gin and tonic out of a thermos. After the picnic, we all went swimming. Our Cornish holidays had made Jo and me reasonably brave about cold seas, and Mawkie, now at Eton, had to be brave about everything. But Jane, who never swam in Cornwall, got cold very quickly. Perhaps the sun went in? In my memory, everything turned grey and worrying at this point. Jane ran out of the water and dashed to her towel. We all obediently followed. The bathing costume she was wearing, lime green and very tight, was fastened with a zip. As she frantically struggled to get out of this garment, the zip stuck. Shivering and cross, she sent Ivo back to the Bentley to fetch pliers from the car tool kit. Jo, Mawkie and I tried to warm her up with our towels, but she told us not to be silly, our towels were 'soaking'.

Ivo arrived with the pliers. He attacked the zip and eventually got it to move, and my mother tugged on her clothes. But the lime-green bathing costume was torn by the pliers and Jane couldn't prevent herself from becoming angry and tearful. All she wanted now was to go home.

She seemed to forget completely that this was meant to be my birthday treat, that a cake waited in its tin. Did we eat the cake? I can't remember. I knew that not just the lime-green costume was ruined, but the birthday also.

There is something pathetically and hilariously funny about this scene, but it was also wounding.[1] Such is its power that, all my life since then, I've never been able to surrender completely to the idea of enjoying my birthday. The second of August keeps coming round. Sometimes it seems to dawn brightly, but it always makes me agitated. This is very tough on Richard and on my family, who always do their best to make the day good. Often, it *is* good, especially when my little grandchildren can be part of it. But in my heart, I'm looking out for darkening skies, for the sound of the cold sea, for the thing that will sabotage the day — the thing that nobody else has seen.

★   ★   ★

---

[1] A version of these events appears in my novel *Trespass* (2010). Anthony Verey's adored mother, Lal, ruins Anthony's birthday by becoming trapped in a lime-green bathing suit and giving everybody hell because of her own discomfort. It's interesting to me as a writer that I could do no other than make the bathing costume lime green in the *Trespass* narrative. I think it's the acidity of the colour that makes it fit so perfectly into the emotional picture.

Ivo, I think, must have been dismayed by what happened on that Swanage day. When he married Jane, whom he seemed to love very much, he was surely hoping that her anger and selfishness could gradually be lessened by his own acts of kindness.

He tried many things. One of these was to buy a family dog, a black-and-tan miniature dachshund called Boody. Jo, Mawkie and I were willing to love this soft and touching creature, but Boody was a smart dog: he didn't love us back. He knew who his master was, and that was Ivo. The affection between dog and man was such that when Boody eventually died, I was advised by Jane never to mention the death to Ivo. Proud Yorkshireman that he was, he couldn't stand to be seen weeping.

Though it was smaller than Linkenholt, Frilsham Manor needed several hands to maintain it, and Ivo's money was able to provide these. A Spanish couple, Juan and Maria,[1] lived in the house with us. The cooking was shared between our mother and Maria, but what we ate was very English food: oxtail stew, Sunday roasts, steak-and kidney pudding, baked apples. Juan mended things that got broken and sometimes waited at table, wearing a short white coat. Jane was proud of having employed this Spanish pair (a resolution to what she called 'the increasing post-war servant problem', even if she

---

[1] The names of this couple have been changed, for reasons that will become clear later in this narrative.

didn't want Maria to make Spanish food), and appeared to treat them with patience and courtesy. But down the road of time, something terrible was to happen that called into question her whole relationship with them.

Again with Ivo's money, and with her innate good taste in decoration and furnishings, Jane had made Frilsham Manor very beautiful, and she wanted everything kept in a condition she could be proud of when the visitors' book began filling up. Jim Butler's wife came in three days a week to help Maria with the housework.

It troubled me that Mrs Butler spent such a lot of time on her hands and knees, polishing the hall floor. When we came down for breakfast, there she would be, her thin arms making wider and wider arcs with the polishing rags. At Linkenholt, perhaps because we were only there for short stretches of time, I never remember seeing the servants actually performing arduous tasks of this kind; the brass stair rods, for instance, just seemed to stay polished of their own accord. But I can't think of Mrs Butler without remembering her in her attitude of surrender to the parquet floor. In fact, I can't really remember what she looked like standing up. However, what she achieved with her rags and her beeswax polish I can remember very well: the perfumed air of the Frilsham hall gave up a scent so sweet I still dream about it.

For the first few years after we moved to Frilsham, Nan was always invited to stay for part of the holidays. Her presence in the house confirmed the feeling that the worst family

119

sorrows were over. Ivo, I recall, was impeccably kind to her, and she developed an affectionate respect for him. 'Mummy darling,' I once heard her say, 'you know, dear Sir Ivo is much easier to get along with than Daddy was.' And I couldn't help remembering her saying, 'Stay a bit longer, Daddy,' when we finished the last picture story in the nursery in London and how, with a contrite backward glance, Daddy would always refuse.

Nan at age sixty was a country girl now. She adored going on walks to look for birds' nests, to hear thrushes sing, to pick primroses or bluebells or blackberries, to hunt for mushrooms, to have picnic teas in the woods. I remember that on these outings, as we walked up the steep hill towards the Frilsham Woods, I would hold her hand, as if I was still a very young child. On the picnic rug, I'd nudge up close to her. And I think Jo did this, too. We understood that our lives were separating out and that Nan would never be ours again in quite the same way. We had to hold onto her while she was still there.

★　★　★

Tea, in summertime, when it wasn't a picnic, was laid out in a sunny garden room that had been christened 'the ginnery' by Jane, who thought it was a promising space for pre-lunch gin and tonics. It was a pretty place, but plagued by flies from the cattle that were lodged in farm buildings not far from it. Ivo couldn't stand these flies. In consequence, the air of the ginnery

120

(where I don't remember much gin ever being drunk) was always toxic with fly spray called 'Flit'.[1]

I spent long hours in the ginnery. At Crofton Grange, I'd begun piano lessons, and even my mother understood that I'd never play well if I didn't practise in the holidays, so either she or Ivo had bought me an upright piano, which was the most spectacular gift I'd ever had.

Nobody else played. I struggled through scales for hours on end, breathing in Flit, often attempting to work on music far beyond my mediocre skill. (I was particularly anxious to master Rachmaninov's Prelude in C sharp minor, which, with its three deathly opening chords, thrillingly recounts the story of a man being buried alive.) Sometimes Boody would trot out of the house and stand, outraged, hackles up, at the ginnery door, howling at all my wrong notes. I think the poor little dog wanted me to be buried alive. And Mawkie remembers that I used to get in such 'baits' about my own less than marvellous skills at the ginnery piano that he began nicknaming me 'Baitie' — a name for me he still loves to use and which makes us both laugh. ✦

Our piano teacher at Crofton Grange was Joyce Hatto, at that time a rising star on the professional recital circuit. Why she needed to

---

[1] In *Sacred Country*, Mary Ward, unloved by her impecunious father and furiously jealous of her younger brother, Timmy, attempts to kill him by spraying Flit into his bedroom.

spend time teaching at a girls' boarding school I've never completely understood, but we were lucky to have her. Just as Robbie was a true teacher of literature, so Joyce Hatto brought to our piano lessons the musical understanding that can only come from a true talent.

The sound she herself could make on the school Bechstein was impeccably bright. The ends of her slim fingers were bent backwards by their constant caress of the keys. She could sight-read anything and everything, so that she could always show you exactly how the piece you were learning was meant to sound. I was not the only girl to think, sometimes, how I would have preferred my half-hour lesson to be spent just listening to Joyce, instead of enduring my own struggles.

My hands are long-fingered and strong. I could reach an octave with no trouble and my feeling for the music enabled me to put some emotional ballast into stern bass chords. What I could never master was fast-paced accuracy. 'Fingering! Fingering!' Joyce would bleat at my side, as I kept taking wrong pathways from one note to another. And yet she was always encouraging, always gentle. She saw, no doubt, that I would never have any real dexterity as a pianist, but kept me on as her pupil (when some girls were demoted to the second-string music teacher, the hilariously named Miss Elgar) because she understood the ways in which my *head* connected to the mood and feeling the composer had intended, and this interested her.

I realise now that Joyce Hatto was only in her

twenties when she came to Crofton Grange, although at the time she seemed older. She was small and electric, with frizzy brown hair and a fondness for wide skirts, smart court shoes and scarlet lipstick. She did everything fast. The whole pace of our lives at Crofton seemed to speed up whenever she was around. We yearned to please her.

★　★　★

In 1959, when our class were all aged fifteen or sixteen, Joyce Hatto took the enormous risk of arranging a pupils' concert in the recital room at the Royal Festival Hall. Twenty-four of us would perform short pieces. The concert would be open to the public, with tickets priced from seven shillings and sixpence to five shillings. At least fifty of the seven-and-sixpenny seats would be filled with proud parents.

Excitement about this event — so unique in our sheltered, repetitious lives — was colossal. Among my close friends, Jane McKenzie and Elsa, we talked of almost nothing else. We longed for the day to come, not only because we were all going to be stars for five minutes each on 18 July, but because after the recital we were going to be allowed to go out to tea with our families. Visions of salmon-paste sandwiches and chocolate cake found their way only too easily into our minds. This promised to be the best, the most memorable day of our lives.

The first disappointment for me was when Ivo and Jane said they couldn't come to the concert.

123

Perhaps I shouldn't have been surprised. Neither of them had ever had any real relationship to classical music, so they probably worried that this would be an ordeal for them. Either this, or they had planned one of their fishing holidays. I can't remember. Everybody else received rapturous letters from their parents telling them how proud they were that we were going to perform in this prestigious London venue. But Jane had never done 'proud'. The things I achieved down the years never quite got the response I'd hoped for.[1]

Disappointed here, my friends encouraged me to write to Keith, whom I hadn't seen for years, and ask him if he would come. I remember thinking that this was a waste of time; he would certainly say no. He and Virginia had made it clear that he would take no interest in his first family. By now, he had four more children and a life that had no room in it for us. What I did remember, however, was him playing the piano in the library at Linkenholt.

---

[1] This refusal to take seriously my first productions and publications as a writer caused me more grief than I wanted to admit. I got used to it. But when my first BBC radio play, *The Wisest Fool*, described as a 'lollapalooza of a play' by Bill Ash, the assistant head of radio drama, was broadcast in April 1976 as an Afternoon Theatre production, and Jane told me she wouldn't be able to listen as she was going to a lunch party, 'which I can't very well cut short', I felt the sting of this response. It still strikes me as unimaginative.

To my then unpractised ear, I'd guessed that he played well. He'd always seemed relaxed and calm when seated at the Linkenholt Blüthner. And this suggested that music-making might possibly be something that still interested him. So I decided to send the letter. And when the reply came, saying that he would definitely be there, I think I may have wept with a kind of joyful shock.

★  ★  ★

The piece I was to play at the recital was Rimsky-Korsakov's 'Song of India', a nice slow, melodic number, well chosen by Joyce as being right for both my technical limitations and my emotional strengths. My slot would be in the first half of the event. The stars of our group, Caroline Gee and Elisabeth von Petersdorff, would be saved until last. Joyce herself would wind up the recital with a Chopin prelude.

We were driven to London on a coach, all of us sick with excitement and fear. The day was hot. I can remember the dress I wore, with a patterning of coral-coloured tulips on a white background. My 'useless' hair was now cut very short, the better to be tamed and organised.

Our first sight of the Festival Hall, that great modernist concrete edifice built to celebrate the Festival of Britain in 1951, and the knowledge that we were actually going to be inside it, performing in the recital room, cast us into a stunned silence. Backstage with Joyce, who paced around on her court shoes, encouraging us with her bright voice, we tried to calm our nerves by peering through a tiny space in the curtains, to see the parents arriving.

When I saw Keith — looking just the same as when I'd last seen him — I had difficulty believing that I wasn't hallucinating. He'd become so ghostly in my mind that the physical fact of his presence felt unreal. But Jane McKenzie, who had known him since the days of Miss Vista's dancing class, clutched my arm excitedly and said, 'It's him, Rosie. It's definitely him!'

It was him.

He stayed to hear my performance, which Joyce reassured me had gone well, but when we looked through the curtains again after the interval, the seat my father had occupied was empty.

★ ★ ★

The second half of the concert began. I kept looking and looking, staring at the empty chair, but Keith never reappeared. No doubt he felt bored by the idea of sitting through the efforts of another ten or twelve anxious girls. No doubt he'd forgotten about the promise of tea. But the realisation that, although he'd seen me on the stage, he couldn't be bothered to wait to say hello to me was wounding.

The next thing I remember is standing by myself near the river, outside the Festival Hall. The sun was still hot, sparkling on the then-drab wharves of the South Bank and the muddy Thames. The other girls were going off to tea with their parents and I was alone. I remember wondering if I was being punished for neglecting

126

to invite Nan, who would have applauded ridiculously loudly when I came on in my tulip dress, whose smile I would have been able to feel as my 'Song of India' unfolded into life.

But why hadn't I invited her? Had there been a 'parents only' edict from the school, just as there was on parents' days? Had I been worried that Nan might take the wrong bus and get lost on her way to the great concert hall? Whatever the truth or otherwise of all this, I was now sick with misery.

Loyal Jane McKenzie came and found me and I was taken to tea with her and her parents, Pam and Malcolm. Pam McKenzie said to me, 'I always liked your father, Rosie dear, because he amused me. He used to call me 'Pam-Pam', after a French variety of tinned tomato juice — and that made us all laugh. But today he was a shit.'

**ROYAL FESTIVAL HALL**                    **RECITAL ROOM**
General Manager : T. E. Bean, C.B.E.

**Saturday, 18th July, 1959 at 3 p.m.**

THE FORWARD MUSIC GROUP

Presents a

# RECITAL BY PUPILS OF
# JOYCE HATTO

Susan Atkins; Juliet Attenborough; Elizabeth Blackadder; Elsa Buckley; Caroline Eley; Alison Fairfax-Lucy; Elizabeth Fogg Elliot; Caroline Gee; Fiona Gillespie; Marilyn Gillespie; Heather Gray; Margaret Hedges; Juliet Locks; Sonia Locks; Cynthia Mackenzie; Jennifer Marrow; Jane McKenzie; Susan Merrick; Susan Patchett; Elisabeth von Petersdorff; Jane Riches; Gillian Sheppard; Virginia Thompson-McCausland; Rosemary Thomson.

Programme includes Works by
BACH, MOZART, BEETHOVEN, SCHUBERT, CHOPIN, LISZT, GRIEG, DOHNANYI, MOSZKOWSKI, RACHMANINOFF

TICKETS : 7/6 and 5/- from Box Office, Royal Festival Hall Telephone: WATerloo 3191

VAIL & CO. LTD., LEEKE STREET, LONDON, W.C.I

127

A different kind of music now started to be played at Frilsham — the music of adolescent love: Ella Fitzgerald and Frank Sinatra, Elvis Presley and the Everly Brothers.

Jo had left school to study art at the Académie Julien in Paris, but Jane and Ivo allowed Mawkie and me to link up with Berkshire friends, and a round of teenage parties, known as 'hops', began. We would be driven to these hops in Ivo's Rover (the Bentley had gone by this time — an early sign, perhaps, that his money was not going to last for ever), and he and Jane would spend the evening drinking and playing Scrabble in a nearby pub before collecting us at around eleven o'clock.

This, it now strikes me, was quite generous of them. The only time Ivo would not drive was if there was any suggestion of mist or fog, and Mawkie and I missed quite a few parties because of this. Sometimes we would be only two or three miles from the party and Ivo — to our great disappointment and teenage fury — would turn back. Richard has recently suggested to me that Ivo's extreme fear of these weather conditions probably dated from his wartime experience in the Royal Air Force and his understanding of how so many flying accidents occur because of poor visibility, and I think he may be right.

I fell in love with a boy called Dermot Halloran. I was fifteen. He was seventeen and about to become a cadet at Pangbourne Nautical College. One of my friends from school, Venetia Quarry, was in love with Dermot's brother, Mike. Hilarious letters were exchanged between me and Venetia on the subject of the Halloran brothers. I kept them for years in a blue plastic folder and would love to be able to quote accurately remembered lines like 'Has D X'd you properly yet?'

Dermot Halloran was tall and dark, with beautiful skin and a pouty expression that reminded everybody of Elvis. Even Jane admitted he was 'a bit of a dish'. It was at this time that she bought me my first pair of high-heeled shoes, and she was amused, I think, by the teenage crushes Mawkie and I were now unable to hide. Perhaps she suddenly understood, to her profound relief, that we were children no longer; that the end of our parental dependency was just within sight.

The best of the teenage hops was one we gave at Frilsham. Jane laid this on very well, with a fairly innocent wine cup for us to drink and a carefully planned cold buffet set out in the dining room. I wore my new high heels and a dress of blue-green taffeta. After supper, we put on our music and danced on the polished parquet of the hall.

This event had about it a kind of magic. All my closest friends were there, about twelve or fourteen of them, including the Halloran brothers and my cousin Johnny. We turned off all the lights, and in the soft darkness of the hall we paired off and clung to each other, danced, jived, kissed, touched and dreamed. Now and then Ivo would come barging in (from where he and Jane sat playing Scrabble in the ginnery) and turn the lights back on, but as soon as he'd gone, we turned them off again. All teenagers endure

129

difficult times, but this night was beautiful; it was entirely ours.

It's interesting to remember what became of all this collective first love.

In my case, I went back to school and Dermot Halloran went to Pangbourne Nautical College. We saw each other at parties in the holidays for about a year, exchanging chaste kisses. Then he left the country to join the Canadian navy.

Venetia and Mike Halloran also split up and Venetia, pushed by her mother, Lady Mancroft, soon embarked on a fierce and successful pursuit of a rich husband, which she eventually found in Fred Barker, a young man so rich he was able to buy a large house in Hampshire, pull it down and build an even larger one in its place. Clearly the Halloran family had not been nearly rich enough.

The only serious (because sexually consummated) love was between a clever boy called Robin Peat, who was just coming to the end of a starry career at Eton, and my very beautiful friend Nancy Phillpotts, cousin of my class-mate, Julie. Nancy, aged sixteen, told us all at school that she was going to marry Robin. She described her stays in Norfolk with his family as 'honeymoons'.

Then Robin was snatched away from her. When he unexpectedly failed his Oxford entrance exam, his disappointed parents packed him off to Europe, to recover from this setback. In Italy, he met a young Greek student called Cathy. Having so passionately deflowered Nancy, he was of course going to deflower Cathy, too.

No young girl resisted Robin Peat, and he knew it. He quickly made Cathy pregnant and was obliged to forget Nancy — his 'Nou' as he called her — and marry Cathy in a Greek Orthodox ceremony we hated to hear about.

Poor Nou. Poor Robin.

Miraculously, Nancy and Robin met again decades later in Paris. Nancy's Austrian husband, Hanni, had died. Robin divorced his second wife and married his long-lost Nou. But he was a disappointed man by then, all his early promise seemingly gone. Together Nancy and Robin embarked on buying and running a wine business at Château l'Eperon near Bordeaux — Robin's last fling at living the life he wanted with the girl he'd always loved. But the business was too arduous for them. Robin died of alcoholism in 2004.

# Milton's Oppositions

Hence, loathed Melancholy,
Of Cerberus and blackest midnight born
In Stygian cave forlorn,
'Mongst horrid shape, and shrieks and sights
 unholy,
Find out some uncouth cell,
Where brooding darkness spreads his jeal-
 ous wings,
And the night-Raven sings;
There, under Ebon shades and low-brow'd
 rocks
As ragged as thy locks,
In dark Cimmerian desert ever dwell . . .

These lines, from John Milton's *L'Allegro*,
became engraved into my mind in my O-level
exam year at Crofton Grange. We were studying
the lyric poems *L'Allegro* and *Il Penseroso* as
part of our syllabus, enduring, no doubt, some
struggle with Milton's classical allusions, which
are strewn about like boulders in the river of the
poems, but helped here by Robbie's perpetual
cry: 'Look it up! Look it up!'

At some point in the year, Robbie came to me
and asked if I would consider attempting a large
mural, illustrating scenes from *L'Allegro* and *Il
Penseroso*, for the upper panel of the English
room wall. She said she disliked the drabness of
the room, in which she had to spend so many

hours, had wanted something 'permanent' done about it for a long time, and now it had come to her that she had found the perfect subject for the painting.

Robbie warned me that 'like Michelangelo in the Sistine Chapel' I would be working high up, but scaffolding towers would be brought in and strong boards laid between them, so that I would be quite safe while I painted. To prepare for this big enterprise, I would submit drawings to her, done on graph paper so that they could be scaled up correctly onto the wall. The choice of imagery would be mine, but the overall design would have to have a classical unity about it and be approved by Robbie before I began.

She wanted this done in one term. As I acquired the graph paper and began preliminary sketches, I remember worrying about fitting in my O-level revision around the hours I would be spending on the scaffolding. I wanted to rise to the challenge of Robbie's mural, but I didn't want to fail my exams. I discussed my dilemma with my closest friends, Jane, Elsa, Alison Fairfax-Lucy and Heather Gray, and they solved it for me by suggesting that we would all get up at five in the morning through the rest of the term and put in two hours' revision before breakfast.

This we did. To our own surprise, we stuck at it. And I remember that those early May mornings, with the sunrise casting soft shadows onto the park, with the extreme quiet that pervaded the building, had something beautiful about them. Part of the beauty lay, I think, in the secret feeling that, by doing this unseen work, we were putting ourselves ahead of everybody else. There was now no chance that our little group would fail our O-levels. Our brains were being crammed at dawn. Even Jane McKenzie, who couldn't draw very well, was helped to perfect biologically correct sketches of sprouting broad beans and brown water beetles. Part of every revision session was given over to talking to each other in hilariously hopeless French, as prep for the French oral exam. We passed around mapping pens, atlases, compasses, dictionaries and oranges. The taste for academic work, pure and undiluted, was born in me on those early mornings.

My sketches for the Milton mural proliferated and improved. Robbie's mention of Michelangelo led me, with excruciating vanity, to see myself in his heroic light. For hours and hours I studied his drawings and paintings of the human body. Though Milton's poems are crowded with images of the natural world, and I knew that 'dappled dawn', 'sweet briar', 'russet lawns', 'elms and hillocks green' as well as 'antick pillars' and 'cloysters pale' had to form the background to the work, I also needed to paint shepherds, milkmaids, pensive nuns, muses, bards, kings and gods. Enthralled by Michelangelo's capture of the massive human form in fluid movement, I slowly assembled my group of figures around the personification of Melancholy itself, a brooding male figure in Puritan dress, resting his chin on a languid, Michelangelesque hand.

How many hours did it take me to execute this mural? I remember that I worked through other classes' lessons, trying to keep as quiet as I could, and that I was 'excused knitting' for that term and so could go there for an hour after lunch, when everyone else was struggling with their charity garments. Just the squaring up of the wide panel took me a long time. I would have been helped by good maths, but this subject had dripped off my school agenda at age fourteen.

I worked in oil paints, which I'd never used before, but for which I became grateful. With watercolours, and to a certain extent with the poster paints we used in our art classes, the execution has to be right at the first attempt, but with oils you can indulge in what the Old Masters called 'pentimento', obliterating one image by putting another on top of it. I think there must have been a lot of pentimento in that huge mural. As I recall it, the central figure, which owed so much to my study of the Sistine Chapel paintings, had a powerful presence. Most of the larks, roosters and nightingales flew or strutted around in a touching and companionable way, but I remember that some of the shepherdesses, and even some of the gods themselves, looked a bit dead on the wall.

Robbie would come and visit me frequently, stare up at the work slowly taking shape and be honest about its perceived weaknesses, which I would then struggle to correct. But she and I also talked about other things. She would sit under my ladders and we would discuss the way in which Milton, writing these poems at a young age, already understood so well the way the human mind is poised between its longing for what he calls 'vain deluding joyes' and its deep

135

attraction to melancholy, so fatally bright in the mind's eye that it has to mask itself with 'black staid Wisdom's hue'.

I remember telling Robbie that she'd found the right artist to interpret this idea, that my own mind, though capable of rejoicing, was almost insatiably drawn to tragic contemplation. I admitted to her that when we'd embarked on *Romeo and Juliet* in my first year (and in the wake of finding myself cast away from so much that I'd known and loved), what I responded to in it was the 'absolute total sadness of it'.[1]

These musings brought the familiar, toothy smile onto Robbie's creased face. Our discussion of the work in hand and the emotions behind it led on, at some stage, to ideas about my future.

Robbie had assumed, and so had I, that I would stay on at Crofton Grange for the A-level years and that my ultimate target would be a place at Oxford. Robbie evoked her own time there, before the war, and how privileged she'd

---

[1] I decided to give this perception of *Romeo and Juliet* to Lewis Little, the fourteen-year-old protagonist of my 1997 novel, *The Way I Found Her*, and this felt completely right for him. The adolescent sensibility that finds the sadness of the play so alluring is the one drawn so fatally and irrevocably to Valentina Gavril, a passionate Russian writer of 40. When, late in the novel, Lewis and Valentina endure captivity together and begin a sexual relationship, it is primarily their response to affliction and sorrow that binds them.

felt to be among the very few women taking undergraduate degrees. I longed to follow her there. She convinced me that I would 'fit in' at Oxford and be happy in its intense environment. She was prepared to use any contacts she had to help me get there. She warned me only to work harder at Latin, the one subject where my grades were poor. 'There is plenty of time,' she said, 'but we have to start planning now.'

Excited by this, I dropped the magic word 'Oxford' into letters sent home at this time, but then noticed that this never elicited any comment. I assumed that my mother and Ivo felt it was too soon — prior to O-levels — to be discussing university. Yet this ignoring of the subject was disconcerting. In Robbie's presence, it was so easy to conceive a clichéd picture of myself already there, cycling along the Broad with copies of *Paradise Lost* and *Hamlet* in a wicker basket, with clever new friends by my side. I imagined entertaining Robbie, toasting her favourite marshmallows in front of the gas fire in my rooms, going with her to visit John Masefield. But it was not long before I understood that my mother had other ideas for me. She wanted me further away than Oxford. She was planning a different path.

⋆ ⋆ ⋆

Meanwhile, something terrible had happened to her.

I have no record of the exact date when this thing was revealed to me, only that it coincided

137

with my time spent working on the Milton mural. Rapt by my early-morning studies, by my hours spent pretending to be Michelangelo, I'd achieved a happiness and an equilibrium at Crofton Grange I'd never thought possible. But meanwhile, my poor mother was being taken apart by an absolutely unlooked-for event.

I first heard about it in a letter from Ivo. In his fluent, unshaky writing, he alluded to an 'attack' on Jane by Juan and Maria. He said that the Spanish couple had immediately been sacked and that Jane was recovering in hospital.

Ivo gave no details. He reassured me that everything was going to be all right — that she had been 'saved' by Jim Butler, who was working in the garden when the attack happened and heard her screams and came rushing to her aid.

I found it difficult to imagine this scene. Juan and Maria had been with us for several years and had seemed happy at Frilsham. That they could have attacked Jane didn't seem likely at all. Jo was away in Paris and perhaps wasn't informed about this at the time, in case her studies at the Académie Julien were disturbed. And when Mawkie and I came home for half term, we were told by Ivo not to mention a word about it, in case we upset Jane, who was now out of hospital but needed everybody's loving care.

Mawkie and I puzzled over the drama. A temporary cook had replaced Maria, but Jane still spent part of each morning in the kitchen, part of the summer days doing her 'little bits' in the garden, with which we now tried to help her. Things seemed pretty much normal. There were no visible physical wounds on Jane's body. There were one or two unexplained overheard conversations. I remember Mawkie saying to me, 'Fuck, Baitie! I heard the words 'going to court'! Is there going to be a trial, or something?'

There were a thousand questions we wanted to ask, as no doubt Ivo understood, but we weren't allowed to ask them. Secrecy and silence were the watchwords Ivo and Jane had chosen. But eventually we found out from Jane herself what had happened.

This was rape.

Ivo had been away in York, where he still held some directorships that demanded a few days of his time. On the fatal afternoon, Jane had gone into her bedroom for a nap, with her curtains drawn. Her bedroom door was unlocked.

Soon afterwards, Juan and Maria had come into the room. They went to the bed and held Jane down. Juan attempted to rape Jane, while Maria looked on. Jane began screaming, but Maria covered her mouth with her hand, so in fact Jim Butler *didn't* hear those screams. The rape took place and it was only after Juan and Maria had gone out of the room that Jane was able to pick up the telephone and call Jim's cottage.

Jim and his wife came rushing to the house, whose front door was seldom locked at that time. They comforted Jane as best they could and called the police. The police arrested Juan and Maria. Ivo was contacted and immediately began the long drive back from York.

What happened next? When Jane related all

this to me, she said that both Ivo and the police encouraged her to bring a court case against Juan and Maria, but that she didn't want to do it. Her fear of having this humiliating and traumatic event 'spread all over the newspapers' overwhelmed her desire for justice. She no doubt felt that terrifying mix of anger and shame that afflicts all rape victims, but she couldn't see any way forward in her life at that point except to try to put it out of her mind and move on. She probably decided on this course of action as much for our sakes as for her own. Juan and Maria were released without charge, but what became of them after that I never found out.

How much did this incident affect Jane's state of mind?

I think it's a credit to Ivo and his gentle care of her that — to us, at least — she seemed just about the same: generous and thoughtful at times, very often impatient and severe, tormented by stomach ailments, quick to anger but also capable of being delighted and amused by her world of close friends, bridge parties and fishing holidays. In some obstinate core of herself, Jane was a survivor. She'd survived an unloved childhood, the death of her brothers and desertion by my father. Now she'd been raped by a trusted servant. No doubt this devastating afternoon returned to her frequently in her dreams. I think it probably put her off sex for ever: she and Ivo had separate rooms from this time onwards. But she didn't give in to hatred or self-loathing; she just carried on.

But *why* had this happened? Had Juan and

Maria nurtured a secret hatred for Jane across months and months? Had she ever wounded them with an angry physical slap, the way that she'd wounded me in Liberty's? There must have been something. But what? Because Maria was party to the repulsive crime, they must have planned it together. It must have been overwhelmingly exciting to them, sexually, with risk as part of the thrill. But how did they think they were going to get away with it? Had they relied on the possibility that Jane's feelings of shame and disgust would prevent her from ever speaking about it, even to Ivo?

When she was old, I once tried, very tentatively, asking Jane about it. She stared at me in bewilderment, as though she couldn't imagine what on earth I was talking about. Then she sent me away. She said she was tired and needed to be left alone to sleep.

★　★　★

I returned to Crofton Grange. The Milton mural was finished. Exams were upon us. We passed them, as we knew we would, all except Latin, which had been badly taught by a short-tempered woman aptly named Miss Gaul, and which none of us had taken seriously enough. I reassured Robbie I would resit the Latin exam the following year. But the following year never came.

In the midst of the O-level weeks, I sometimes went into the English room and stared critically at the wall, now so crazy with flowers, showers, bowers and towers. I knew Robbie had, in the end, been pleased with it. I'd been rewarded with a few celebratory visits to her room, where we toasted marshmallows in front of her gas fire, and talked about Milton's *Lycidas*, which was one of Robbie's favourite poems.

For Lycidas is dead, dead ere his prime,
Young Lycidas, and hath not left his peer.
Who would not sing for Lycidas?

Indeed, who would not? My early affection for this work became in my half-formed mind almost as great as that for *Romeo and Juliet*, not only for its lyric desolation, for the sweet memory of Robbie's recitations, but also because the countryside evoked in it, the 'high lawns', the 'self-same hill', segued in my mind into Linkenholt, my paradise lost.

Robbie had also recommended that my labours be rewarded by something called the Good Citizenship Cup — about which I was mercilessly but good-naturedly teased by my friends. But I wasn't totally sure I'd earned the marshmallows, or the cup. I felt that the only bit of the mural that had value was the central figure, with its brooding face and well-drawn hands. The rest seemed amateurish and weak to me. Not for the first time, I thought how much better the whole thing would have been if it had been executed by Jo.

Jo, in Paris, was now experiencing her first encounter with love, falling for Paul, the forty-year-old son of the Frenchwoman she

142

lodged with on the Avenue Victor Hugo. She was nineteen. And she felt so torn between the passion that she felt for Paul and her fear of the sexual act and its consequences that she felt stranded, as though on some terrible ice floe, in a sea of confusion. All she could do was call for help. Jane and Ivo rushed over to Paris, extracted Jo from the Académic Julien (where she had been doing well, bringing home some beautiful watercolours of the great City of Light), and from the Avenue Victor Hugo — where the middle-aged Paul, still tied to his mother's apron strings, nevertheless felt something more than paternal tenderness for Jo — and brought her back to the tranquil green fields of Berkshire.

It's interesting to reflect upon what happened to her next — to this star of my childhood, the girl my parents' friends dubbed 'the talented one'. After the Paris debacle and a period at home, where she painted in a lovely little studio Ivo had kitted out for her in one of the Frilsham outbuildings, she was accepted at the Central School of Art in London, where she was steered away from illustration towards design.

Design was not where Jo's talent lay. Her tutors at Central must have been slightly obtuse not to see this. In a sense, her art school years were wasted, in pursuit of something she couldn't do well. But after this, she returned to her skill with small drawings, pastels and watercolours, working freelance for Gordon Fraser, designing greeting cards. Had she pushed a little harder, found an agent, planned the way ahead, she would surely have found work as an

143

illustrator of children's books.

But after a few years, she stopped it all. Aged twenty-three, she married an advertising copywriter, John Pitt, converted to the Roman Catholic Church at his request, gave birth to six children and never revisited the skill that had defined her childhood and all our expectations. I have always had to respect Jo's decision to set aside a blazing talent, but I have never been completely reconciled to this squandering of something precious.

★   ★   ★

My own turn to be steered away from a planned pathway was approaching.

Before my last term at school had ended, I was told by Jane that Oxford was an 'inappropriate dream', that she didn't want a 'bluestocking' for a daughter. This would make her a laughing stock. Did I want her to be a laughing stock?

'Fuck, Baitie!' Mawkie said to me. 'That's so unfair. What's this 'laughing stock' shit? You've always been bloody brilliant and I was looking forward to coming and seducing your friends at Oxford.'

'Exactly,' I said. 'Exactly, Mawkie. I was looking forward to that too.'

My cousin Johnny was about to sit the Cambridge exams, and Rob would soon be destined for Oxford. But for me, 'the bluestocking', it was not to be. Resistance to what Jane had planned felt impossible. I was leaving Crofton Grange and being sent abroad to a 'finishing school' in Switzerland. That was the term for the place my mother wanted to consign me to: a 'finishing school'.

I wept tears with Robbie under my brooding incarnation of Melancholy. My vision of myself at Oxford was still unbearably vivid. Robbie offered to write a 'strong letter' to my mother. But I told her it was a waste of time. I told her I could do nothing else but submit. And this is one of the enduring mysteries of my childhood: why didn't I stand up to Jane? Why didn't I argue and shout? I had moments of hating her with a profound, deep-seated dislike, and yet I never seemed to have the courage to challenge her rulings — not even her ruling against Oxford. The nearest I can get to explaining this is that, in some way, I was terrified of her. Later in my life, Johnny and Robert admitted that they'd been afraid of her too. Retrospectively, Johnny christened her 'the Godmother'. He'd watched appalled as everybody jumped to do her bidding.

So then, I reason that, though years may pass, lovelessness can lay the seeds of tyranny. The tragic, rejected 'Little Dudley' was, in her middle years, a despotic woman: 'Little Corleone'.

★   ★   ★

During my last term at Crofton Grange, 1959, Joyce Hatto was giving her first orchestral concert with the London Symphony Orchestra at the Festival Hall and arranged tickets for a group of her pupils.

Jane and Ivo never took us to concerts, so this

145

was my first entry into the main auditorium at the Festival Hall, and I remember feeling so awed by it that I became breathless and wondered if the air inside was 'different air'. The knowledge that Joyce was going to come walking onto the stage and sit down at the enormous shining piano was almost too overwhelming to contemplate.

The piece she was going to play was Gershwin's *Rhapsody in Blue*, a marvellous, fast-paced show-off number for an adroit pianist, but as the orchestra assembled, our little group fell silent. We worried that, despite the genius she displayed to us at school, our darling Miss Hatto might be overcome by the occasion and suddenly stumble — or worse. Caroline Gee, head of music at Crofton during our time there, told us that she had attended a recital during which Joyce had suddenly fallen into a faint, with her head crashing down onto the keys. What if this terrible occurrence was going to happen again, this time in the huge auditorium of the Festival Hall?

On she came.

We recognised her footfall in her court shoes before we saw her. She wore a long blue taffeta gown. She was smiling her lipsticked smile.

I think we held onto each other as Joyce settled at the piano and started adjusting the stool. Then the first slow laid-back, jazzy bars began. Here, the pianist has to wait and wait . . . wait and wait . . . then pounce. Timing and speed is all, and Joyce was right on it. We stopped worrying and just sat back to marvel.

146

When the piece reached its end, we were tearful with pride. She was *our* Joyce Hatto, and rumours had reached us down the years that she was a star — but now we knew it for sure.

In my recollection, she had a fine ovation from the Festival Hall audience, but of course I *would* remember it like that. This was my first encounter with what we might call fame. Later critics suggested that Joyce Hatto had never been 'in the first rank' of concert pianists. But for me, on this great occasion, the idea that one person (somebody you knew, somebody who otherwise went about her life doing ordinary things) might be good enough, bold enough at something to stir hundreds or thousands of people to strong emotion seemed suddenly quite extraordinary.

★　★　★

Recently, from Caroline Gee, I heard a significant story of something that happened to Joyce during her time as our teacher.

Joyce stayed one night a week at the school, giving lessons on two successive days. It was Caroline's task to wake her up in the morning with a cup of tea well before school assembly, at which we always sang a hymn and Joyce would play the accompaniment.

One morning, over the tea, Joyce suddenly told Caroline that her agent, William Barrington-Coupe, always known as 'Barry', had proposed to her. Joyce said that she hadn't thought about marriage and didn't particularly want to marry Barry, but he'd been sitting at his desk,

147

nervously playing with a yellow toy duck, as he uttered the words of the proposal, and this sight of him anxiously fussing with the duck had seemed so 'pathetic' that Joyce agreed to become his wife, out of sheer pity and sorrow. She married him in 1956.

Much later, long after she had renounced all her teaching in favour of concert performance, a massive musical scandal overtook Joyce Hatto and William Barrington-Coupe. As well as being Joyce's agent, Barry was also a music producer, adept at studio recording and editing. When Joyce developed stomach cancer in the 1990s and became too ill to play to her former standard, Barry decided to embark on a ruinous fraud. During her last years, he issued more than one hundred recordings — including the complete Beethoven sonatas, concertos by Rachmaninov, Tchaikovsky, Mendelssohn and Brahms, and some Chopin preludes — passing them off as Joyce's playing and earning widespread critical acclaim for her, with the music world beginning to ask, 'Where has this brilliant pianist been all these years?' But these recordings were not by Joyce. Barry had spliced in the work of other 'lesser known' concert artists and sold hundreds of CDs, all purporting to be recordings by Joyce, on his Concerts Artists record label. When the fraud was revealed, he swore that Joyce had never known about it, and had listened to the music believing she herself had played it. And right up to his death in 2014, he was strangely blithe about what he'd done, claiming that he'd 'harmed no one' and simply acted out of love for his wife.

The strangeness of this story will no doubt fascinate musicologists for a long time to come, it was so singular, risky and odd. But as Joyce's pupil and friend, I just feel very saddened by it. In the 1980s and 1990s, Joyce and I kept in touch from time to time, and I received some marvellous Chopin and Rachmaninov CDs from her. I loved them. The playing seemed flawless to me. To find out that they were not by her, but just part of Barry's shameless deception, was a bitter shock. I wanted to turn back time, to have Joyce come clattering into the school assembly to play the morning hymn, find her sitting by me at the Crofton Bechstein, then see her walking onto the stage in her blue taffeta gown to play Gershwin — and let her stay there, on the great concert platforms of the world, a genius in her own right.

★  ★  ★

After Gershwin, we returned to Crofton. Everything felt sad, wasted. I envied passionately the girls — like Heather Gray, the newly designated head girl — who were staying on in this place where, for a while, I'd felt so outcast and unhappy.

On my last day, I went to Robbie's room to say goodbye to her. The July day was cold and she'd lit her gas fire. She didn't want to look at me. She picked up her small brass toasting fork and said: 'Shall we cook one last marshmallow?'

★  ★  ★

My final school report, an unusual survivor of the archive of my teenage years, gives out A or A-grades for everything except Latin and gymnastics, in which it's suggested that 'harder work is needed'. The report ends, in Mrs Baines's familiar green ink, with the observation that 'Rosemary is an exceptionally gifted girl', and expresses her sorrow that the school was losing me 'at such an early age'. I was not yet sixteen.

The convention with school reports was that they were sent to the parents, who saw them before we did. Thus Jane had been able to read the report before she had to show it to me. When I got it, I was startled to find it slightly defaced. Ignoring the A grades and the praise from Elizabeth Baines, my mother had scrawled over the 'harder work is needed' gym report, writing, 'Ha! Ha!' and signing it with her formal initials, V.M.T.

# 'Tits to the Valley'

Jane had got rid of us all now.

Carol was working in London, Jo was at the Central School of Art, Mawkie had joined the Fleet Air Arm (where he was destined to become the youngest jet fighter pilot the Fleet Air Arm had ever sent into the skies). And I was sent to Switzerland to my 'finishing school'.

As Jane saw me off on the boat train to Dover, surrounded by a posse of nicely dressed sixteen-year-old girls but nobody that I knew, I couldn't help remembering the story Lois Crane had told me about my mother and Pam McKenzie linking arms as the train to Braughing pulled away and rejoicing that they could now 'get on with life'. Now, I asked myself not what life Jane had to get on with — I knew what her days consisted of; I asked myself what kind of life I was speeding towards.

All lives have moments where, often without warning, the pathway you thought you were on suddenly veers away from its expected direction, or narrows and runs out, and you feel lost. This was what I experienced on my journey to Switzerland: a feeling of profound disorientation. And some anger. I hadn't asked to be sent to Crofton Grange after my father left us, but thanks to my friends, thanks to the drama studio and the teaching of art, thanks to Robbie and Joyce Hatto, I'd managed to put in place the structures of a creative existence there. I'd begun to thrive and feel happy. Now, like poor, confused Alice, I'd been snatched away from all that and was being pushed and shoved through some other unfamiliar door, some stupid new rabbit hole.

★   ★   ★

What waited for me was a collection of solid buildings in the town of Morges, on Lac Léman, gathered together as the school known as 'Mon Fertile'.

This — with its startlingly mockable name — had been founded by a dynamic English-French female couple, Miss Allen and Mademoiselle Clara. I think they — or the school, anyway — owned a massive amount of Swiss real estate. In winter, the whole thing transferred itself to the ski resort of Les Diablerets, where we lived in three large chalets. In both places, the houses were warm and well maintained. At Morges there was also a barn that had been converted into a theatre. How Clara and Allen had come by all this property, we never quite knew.

The house I was allocated to was called Tournesol (Sunflower). It was early autumn and the weather was very beautiful, with the trees just beginning to yellow on the shores of the lake. I was to share a room with two South African girls, Carol Reunert and Jenny Lowe, and I remember being instantly glad about this. I liked the flatness of their accents; liked the fact that they'd come from a different kind of childhood

152

from mine. There was something a bit exotic about them, living in this hot, troubled, black/white country, and this broke through the very English self-pity I was feeling. With them, it seemed possible to set aside my anger with my mother, and hear instead about life in the leafy suburbs of Johannesburg, where Carol and Jenny's families lived, about braais (barbecues), bioscopes (drive-in movies) and the bundu, the great wilderness that still covered so much of South African soil.

There was one primary rule at Mon Fertile: you had to speak French — and only French — from morning to night. This meant, in our first weeks there, that about fifty per cent of our utterances were faulty or absolutely meaningless. The school housed Germans, Dutch, Scandinavians, South Africans, Canadians, Australians and Brits. Each of us torturing the French language in our own particular way, we found ourselves inhabiting a kind of Tower of Babel. The Dutch and the Germans — no surprise here — spoke better French than the rest of us. My French O-level and the lost conversations of our early-morning revision sessions seemed completely inadequate to the task we were being set. But there was no let-up in the rules. At supper, every girl in turn had to stand up and admit the number of words she had spoken in any other language than French. Mademoiselle Clara called this method of teaching a '*baptême du feu*'. We would get burned, we were told, but we would 'soon learn'. There was no other way.

At night, of course, in our room in Tournesol,

153

we could whisper in our own language. And it was during these whispered conversations that Carol Reunert (who was to become a lifelong friend) told me about the disturbing constructs of her life.

Her mother had died when Carol was very young. Her father, Mike, had then married a second time. His bride was called Liz, and — 'Wait for this, Jenny, wait for this, Rosie,' said Carol, 'because it's really shocking and I'm not meant to talk about it' — Liz Reunert had once been married to the notorious murderer Neville Heath.

At that time, Neville Heath was almost as feared in the collective imagination as the Notting Hill serial killer John Christie. Heath and Liz had had a son, Bertie, now Carol's stepbrother, before Heath was hanged in 1946. Neville Heath had savagely murdered at least two women, Margery Gardner and Doreen Marshall, in both cases lashing their flesh with a riding whip and biting off their nipples before bludgeoning them to death.

How had Liz escaped? Carol told Jenny and me all she knew, which was that Liz had once, allegedly, been tied to a tree and whipped, but had managed to distract her husband, untie her bonds and flee before he harmed her further. She never went back, divorcing the 'lady killer' in 1945. Whipping had been one of the preliminaries to murder, so Liz Reunert might well have become Heath's third victim.

In the hush of the Swiss night, Carol said to me and Jenny, 'I wish she *had* been his bloody

154

victim!' She didn't exactly mean this, but she sincerely disliked Liz, who was bullying towards her, showing affection only to Bertie and then to Tricia, the daughter she went on to have with Mike Reunert. Jane had sent me to Mon Fertile because she didn't want a bluestocking for a daughter, but Liz Reunert had sent Carol away not merely because this kind of education was 'the done thing' in rich South African society of that time, but primarily because she felt jealous of her.

★   ★   ★

Early autumn, the moment of our arrival on the hills and shoreline of Lac Léman, is a fine season. I remember that I found great consolation from how things *looked* in this part of Switzerland; very different from the steep, tilting landscape of Wengen, which Jo and I had experienced with Nan, but beautiful just the same. Perhaps, in a world that once again felt random and wrong to me, I responded to its orderliness.

When the time for the grape harvest, the *vendange*, came around, Mademoiselle Clara and Miss Allen allowed us to spend part of our weekends helping with this. These days, vine farmers bring in massive, clever machines that travel between the rows of vines and literally flay the bunches of grapes off their parent plants. But in 1960, when I was at Mon Fertile, hundreds of temporary workers had to be brought in to pick them by hand. Whether a posse of slightly clumsy teenage girls from countries around the

155

globe was really a useful addition to this task, I'm not entirely sure. (I recalled Grandpop saying: 'Every single task on a farm has a right way and a wrong way to be done, and if you do it the wrong way, then everything and everybody will suffer.') We probably picked grapes in 'the wrong way', but at least we didn't have to be paid.

I spent most of my time in the vine fields sketching. The colours of the landscape — the vine leaves turning yellow and russet, the reddish earth, the grape pickers in their blue overalls, the clear sky shading to turquoise as the evening came on — struck me as being as beautiful as anything painted by Gauguin. Did I also do my bit picking grapes? I suppose so, because I remember that we all got very hot in the fields and on our way back were allowed to buy bottles of apple juice. I can see the dark little shop in Morges even now, with its massive refrigerated cabinets and its pallid lighting. Whenever we could afford it, we also bought 'Swiss yoghurt' — the first yoghurt I'd ever tasted, with bits of apricot and pear whipped into it. Sometimes we could only afford one or two pots between us all, and these got passed and passed around, every spoonful savoured.

★ ★ ★

How else were we 'finished' in that autumn term?

We learned to type. We'd been told that what awaited us, once we'd been 'finished' (and prior to marriage, of course — marriage to a rich man), was secretarial work. We'd work for men who had been educated to be whatever they were capable of being, and we would serve their needs. There was no question of *us* aspiring to *be*. (This was 1960, and feminism had not yet come storming into the world.) We were to facilitate the dreams and ambitions of others, the male of the species.

For this facilitation, learning to type was essential. Mon Fertile would give us 'the rudiments', and we'd then go on to do full-time secretarial courses in our home countries. One hundred words a minute of shorthand (or more if we wanted the 'really interesting' secretarial jobs) was to be our eventual goal. The men would dictate at speed and we'd capture their wise words in clever hieroglyphs.

So that was it, then? That was going to be the limit of my future?

Could it have been true that the parents of all the girls at Mon Fertile — reasonably educated girls from seven or eight countries — had no better aspirations for their daughters, in 1960, than this: that we be assistants to the careers of others, and afterwards their obedient wives?

It was true.

As I sat in the typing classes, echoes of Joyce Hatto bleating, 'Fingering! Fingering!' whipped round my bored and exhausted head. I remember longing to be back at Crofton Grange, seated at the ancient school Bechstein with Joyce, at a moment in my life when so many things appeared possible.

157

★　★　★

Far more interesting than the hours spent bashing away at the ancient Olivettis and Adlers were our French literature classes. We struggled mightily with the plays of Corneille and Racine, which, in their curious formality of language, remained stubbornly inaccessible to us. Shakespeare, so difficult-seeming at first, had yielded to our perseverance, setting down before us a whole universe of new thought, new meaning and new emotion. But Racine and Corneille somehow refused to be approached. We tried to wrestle with them, to *tame* them, but we couldn't. They seemed to be saying to us, 'Listen, barbarians! We are French and we live inside a very ornate château built entirely from learned poetic secrets and conventions. You may come in, if you dare — you who mangle the French language — but you will never have the key to unlock the knowledge of our world that you seek.'

But there were other French authors who were more friendly towards us. The work that meant the most to us in that first term in Switzerland was Antoine de Saint-Exupéry's *Le Petit Prince*, which we read first as a book and then put on as a play.

*Le Petit Prince* is of course a very simple story, more suited to our (improving, but still low) level of discourse in French. It's an allegory for children about vanity, loyalty and death that has captured the hearts of grown-ups for a century. An aviator is forced to land in a desert, a thousand miles from anywhere habitable, where he's visited by a tiny beautiful boy, styling

158

himself a prince, whose home is an asteroid. ('Saint-Ex' himself, a pioneer airmail pilot, had once crashed in the North African desert. Later, he became a wartime pilot, flying observation aircraft out of Corsica. He was killed in 1944.)

The Little Prince has previously dropped in on other miniature worlds, encountering a king, a businessman, a fox, a lamplighter and other eccentrics, and recounts these adventures to the stranded airman. Saint-Exupéry offers a particularly memorable and farcical meditation on the whirling nature of time in the boy's encounter with the lamplighter. The asteroid on which this character lives is so small that mere seconds pass between day becoming night and night again becoming day. Thus the lamplighter's task is endless and without pause: '*J'allume, j'éteins. 'J'allume, j'éteins.*' His world has no other meaning but this.

The Little Prince longs to return to his own star and to the single pampered and fussy rose he has nurtured there. The story's power lies both in the sweetness of the boy and in its startling resolution, whereby the Little Prince must die in order to let his spirit fly home.

In our play, directed by an elderly, clever teacher called Mademoiselle Lelièvre, I was cast as the rose. Perhaps my name suggested it, or perhaps, dressed in the expensive clothes Jane had bought me, I came across as a pampered person. To my amusement, Carol Reunert has called me 'La Rose' for fifty years, and every time she says this, we are both transported to the shores of Lac Léman and our sweet success with our play of *Le Petit Prince*.

It must have been very simply done in the cavernous old barn, but then the set is an empty desert, not the castle of Udolpho. The costumes were simple, too. I wore a green leotard with brown tights and a home-made ruff of cardboard leaves round my neck. I wanted to dye my hair red (captivating idea!), but this wasn't allowed, so I think I wore some kind of scarlet hat — perhaps even a bathing hat, of the kind made fashionable by Elizabeth Taylor, with little rubberised flower petals all over it.

The reason the play succeeded was that our struggles with the words were, somehow, at last overcome. It was the first opportunity we had to *live* something in French. The lines and the acting gradually became one. In my desire to convey both the wilfulness and the vulnerability of the rose, once I'd mastered the lines, I forgot that I wasn't in my own language. And the humour and sadness of the piece, sentimental and quirky though the whole thing is, couldn't fail to move our audience: captive girls being finished before their lives had properly started, and their ageing, slightly sorrowful teachers.

*How many English words have you spoken today? None.*

★   ★   ★

It's interesting to remember that I did no writing at Mon Fertile: not one poem, not one play or story. Nothing.

This is explained, in part, by the fact that I was trying to cram another language into my head.

And I have understood, since that time, how being cut off from English speech affects my work. Writers need to *swim* in a language, like wicked sharks in the deep. Take us out of the ocean of words and we start to die. But I think I also did no writing in Switzerland because part of me had abandoned the whole idea. When I was on my 'Oxford path', with Robbie, taken to tea with John Masefield and confiding my secret hopes to him, it was possible to believe that I really would go forward and achieve some of the things that had eluded my father; that I would be good enough, dedicated enough, thoughtful enough, original, witty and clever enough to be taken seriously as an author. And now, finding myself being 'finished', scrubbed and shined up for a different kind of life as somebody's secretary, somebody's wife, I gave up.

Was there a moment when I consciously turned away from the future I'd nurtured inside my head for so long? Or did I just try to stop thinking about it and let it fade away? I can't remember, but I know some kind of rejection of that imagined 'writer' self took place during my year in Switzerland.

★　★　★

In the winter term, the school moved up to the mountains.

Les Diablerets is now an expensive, crowded ski resort. But it was a village in those days, with a couple of ski lifts, one or two cafés, a fabulous French patisserie shop and a small skating rink. We were housed in three spacious chalets

— fifteen girls to a chalet — and the one I was put in was known as Chardon (Thistle).

Life inside Chardon was presided over by a young teacher called Pierrette Monod. Her physical presence was almost ugly: a very white, round face stippled with dark moles, and a dumpy body. But there was an innocent sweetness about her to which we all responded. In her early twenties, she wasn't so much further through her life than we were, but the thing she liked to tell us, repetitively and endlessly, was that she was already cynical about the world. '*J'ai perdu mes illusions*,' she used to say. The subtext of this was: 'You wait and see, you who are so privileged and blithe, with your rich parents; you will soon understand that the future won't deliver what you hoped for.' I wanted to reply that I already knew this, but I remember having the suspicion that Pierrette's 'lost illusions' were of a more terrible kind than mine, so I kept silent.

Or perhaps I didn't. Pierrette soon had the status of friend.[1] A photograph of the four of us

---

[1] Many years later, I used the physical features of Pierrette Monod for the character of Lydia in *The Road Home* (2007), my novel about immigration and exile. Lydia falls for my protagonist, Lev, on the coach bringing them westwards across Europe, and throughout the novel there is almost no end to the sacrifices she is willing to make for him. But her love remains unrequited. I think there was something slightly tragic about Pierrette that I remembered very vividly when creating Lydia.

— Pierrette, Jenny, Carol and me — eating fondue at Les Diablerets' Café de la Poste seems to confirm how close we all felt to her. Perhaps, on some February evening, with the weight of snow making the roof of Chardon creak, with the darkness outside suggesting the unknown darkness of the life to come, I told her about my lost hopes and the ridiculous future planned for me. Perhaps she told me what sorrows had whipped away those illusions of hers, but if she did, I'm ashamed to say that I can't remember what they were.

★   ★   ★

My friendship with Carol had been cemented in the autumn term, and when the move to Les Diablerets came, we asked if we could share a room. We were informed that our preference could be accommodated, but that there were no double rooms in the chalets, only rooms for three or four. One of the new girls was going to have to be housed with us.

*New girls!*

Carol and I thought ourselves very sophisticated by this time. Our French wasn't bad. We could just about understand the Radio France news bulletins. We'd wrestled with Racine. We'd starred in a play. We'd become favourites of most of the teachers, because we amused them. We could type at twenty-five and a half words a minute. We'd taught each other about make-up and hairstyles. We'd shared the terrible secret about Neville Heath. We didn't want a *new girl,*

163

fresh from her school in England or South Africa. We were 'Carole et La Rose', a fighting duo, making the best of being 'finished', and we didn't want our status disturbed.

When the small posse of new girls descended from the coach outside our chalet, Carol and I knew that we had about thirty seconds to size them up and approach the one we liked the look of best, before she was grabbed by someone else.

She was called Virginia (Ginny) Lathbury. She was the elder daughter of General Sir Gerald Lathbury, who had been wounded during the British Army's daring but ill-fated mission to seize the bridge at Arnhem from the Germans in 1944. Perhaps we saw something of the heroic father in her very sweet face. Then we noticed that her hair was permed, and this made us falter for a split second: could we, who now wore carefully applied black eye make-up, whose role model was Juliette Gréco, share our room with a girl with permed hair?

Yes, we could. (We decided that the perm was indicative of an insensitive mother, not an insensitive girl.) We pounced on Ginny and gave her no choice but to install herself in our chaotic little dorm.

Poor Ginny. Like me, she'd been closeted in a girls' boarding school, Daneshill, for years, then hauled out of it to be finished off in Switzerland. She told me later that Carol and I were not quite what she'd been expecting by way of room-mates: far too boisterous and know-all-ish, far too untidy, far too much Max Factor around the eyes! But she got used to us. She early revealed a

164

lovely sense of humour. She took in her stride her introduction to Piggy, who had crossed Europe with me and now spoke with a low, lugubrious voice to anybody who would listen to him — in both English and French. He was prone to notice life's small difficulties with a sorrowful sigh, and this amused Ginny.

Carol and I concluded that she was a 'good sport'. On that winter's day in 1960, we'd had thirty seconds to select a roommate and we'd chosen well.

★  ★  ★

The main focus of our winter was to learn how to ski. I'd never thought that learning to ski was high on my life's agenda. (No ski runs in Oxford, Jane dear . . . ) But I was now kitted out with the full piste-ready wardrobe and had to give it my best shot.

Our instructor, Monsieur Borloz, was a good-natured man in his forties, tanned from the sun and the ice glare on the snow. The German girls and one or two of the English contingent already knew how to make slalom turns and were taken out of Borloz's group and whisked higher up the mountain in a cable car. We stayed on the nursery slopes, spending long hours of each session stepping sideways upwards to get back to where we could risk a few tentative downhill manoeuvres. Before each run, Monsieur Borloz would remind us that we had to face *outwards*, towards the void. His shorthand for this instruction was 'tits to the valley', which

165

these days sixteen-year-old girls might reasonably object to as sexist mockery, but in 1960
just made us laugh. And throughout my life, with
my family and close friends, 'tits to the valley'
has been used as a hilarious exhortation to
persevere, to confront things head on when times
are bad — a not unhelpful example of the way
humour can defuse fear.

Carol showed an aptitude for skiing from day
one. She had instinctive balance and grace. I had
neither. From the moment I launched myself
down a slope, I felt as though I was destined to
hurtle on, faster and faster, until at last I would
crash into a stand of trees or disappear over
some unseen cliff face. I knew — in theory
— how to make the turns that look so easy when
you watch a good skier executing them. My
left-hand turns felt just about feasible, but
turning to the right — flipping the skis round
with a deft shimmy of the hips — always
appeared to me as something more or less
impossible to achieve, like trying to fly. And you
can't just keep turning left on a ski slope; you'll
soon be facing up the hill and sliding backwards.

There was a lot of frustration in this, as well as
a lot of bruises. I remember reflecting, at this
time, that with so many things I'd attempted in
my sixteen and a half years of life — playing the
piano, typing, riding, playing tennis, skiing — I
always fell short of doing them really, really well.
Even my art — my huge Milton mural — was in
some way less perfect than it should have been.

★   ★   ★

When it came to skiing, Ginny fared even worse than I did.

To get to the nursery slopes from the top of Les Diablerets village, you had to grab a lift, which involved fitting your skis into two grooves in the snow and snatching down a moving plastic seat, attached to an overhead pulley, which you thrust between your legs and it would clamp onto your bottom and drag you upwards.

The inelegant manoeuvre had to be done very fast, or the seat would fly on without you. The most important thing was to watch that your skis didn't come out of the snow grooves, otherwise one or both skis could turn backwards as you were being dragged forwards, and you could break your leg.

On her second day with Monsieur Borloz, Ginny's left ski left the groove and her tibia snapped.

Mountain medics rushed like the shadows of clouds on their skis over the deep snow, and Ginny was taken to hospital on a stretcher that resembled a flat-bottomed red boat. Carol and I kneeled over her, trying to comfort her, but barely able to believe that our new friend, the general's daughter, had been wounded on day two of the battle. It didn't seem remotely fair. Now, not only would she have her permed hair to feel anxious about; her leg would be put into a cast. How could a girl move forward through the winter — move forward through her *life* — with tight curls and tight bandages soaked in plaster of Paris?

Sorrow for Ginny made us kind. When she

came back to Chardon, hopping along on crutches, needing to rest with her leg in the air for part of every day, Carol and I became her only nurses. Pierrette oversaw our ministrations. The other teachers looked in occasionally. Mademoiselle Clara and Miss Allen wrote to Ginny's parents. But we helped her to wash and dress herself. We brought her supper in bed. We sat by her side, trying to make up jokes and stories. We put large rollers in her hair to stretch out the permed curls. Sometimes, in the night, one of us would help her to the lavatory.

Like her father, Ginny was (and remains) a stoic. She was in pain for a long time, far from home, in the company of strangers and a toy pig who kept indulging in insistent commentary of an existential kind, in weather that could turn so bitterly cold that our feet lost all feeling on the skating rink. She cried sometimes, but I don't remember her ever really complaining.

For the rest of us, out on the ski slopes, as winter moved in strange deluding ways towards spring, days of startling sunshine were frequent and our faces soon became as brown as Monsieur Borloz's. We were fit enough from all the sporty exercise, but the food in Les Diablerets was rich and abundant, with an emphasis on cheese pies, veal cutlets and rösti potatoes — irresistible after the mince and cabbage at Crofton Grange — and we ended the year fatter than when we'd begun it.

To compound our weight gain, we were allowed down to the patisserie in the village once a week, where our favourite delicacy was a praline and chocolate confection called a *japonais* — sometimes bought in multiples of four or five. I knew only too well that my mother would dislike the fact that I'd put on weight at Mon Fertile: 'That is a disgusting sight, Rosie!' Extra-tight girdles would no doubt be bought in Newbury. But part of me no longer really cared what Jane thought or desired. When I was sent to Switzerland, the thread that bound us as mother and daughter — always fragile — was becoming badly frayed.

★   ★   ★

Despite never being able to ski really well or perform beguiling little leaps on the skating rink, I wasn't exactly unhappy. I was just *searching*. I remember writing to my father, asking him whether the few moments of transcendent joy I'd experienced walking back from the patisserie in the dusk, through the deep snow, understanding how silence could be such a perfect accompaniment to human existence, were trying to tell me something about the beauty of the world and my future place in it. But realising that his daughter had agreed to be sent to a ridiculous, expensive finishing school, Keith's reaction could only be mocking.

He and Virginia, who now called herself 'Mary' (referred to, with some laughter, by Jane and Ivo as 'Bloody Mary'), had recently become members of a spiritual sect led by the Indonesian guru Muhammad Subuh Sumohadiwidjojo (known as Bapak, or 'Father', Subud), who claimed to have had visions of a seventh or 'highest' heaven. Deep at the heart of this cult, which urged its followers to practise the spiritual exercise Bapak Subud called *latihan*, was a contempt for the material world and those who put their trust in it. Keith (now renamed Stephen, in accordance with Bapak Subud's belief that people had to rename themselves to ascend the spiritual ladder) wrote back to me informing me that the earth was 'the slum of the universe', and that for me to believe that anything important could be conveyed to me by the fleeting beauty of a Swiss mountainside was utterly stupid and pointless.

★ ★ ★

I think this was the last letter I ever wrote to my father.

The pointlessness of everything seemed to break out like a rash all around me. I believe, in retrospect, that the nursing of Ginny — which was very necessary and not pointless at all, but rather laid the foundations for a lifelong friendship — kept me from falling into depression and enabled me to keep alive some kind of hope that my future would have a shape that I could endure and that would lead me onwards — lead me *somewhere*. Yet I couldn't work out where that somewhere was. I knew that it resided in the past, in some composite state of being, where my heart was consoled by Nan's love and my head by a revelation I'd once had in a meadow at Crofton Grange School on a June evening. But these things now felt very far away, receding further and further all the time.

In the quiet of the night at Les Diablerets, in our 'Thistle House', Carol, Ginny and I spent many hours whispering about our futures. But what, really, was there to whisper about? Our childhoods were gone and yet there was nothing much to call us forward into our grown-up lives. A secretarial course. Dull secretarial work, enabling the ambitions of others. Men. Sex. A husband. A white gown.

To me, it didn't seem to be enough.

'Well,' said Carol, 'you'll have to wait and see, La Rose. What else can you do? Just point your tits to the valley.'

# Afterword

So, what happened next?

After Switzerland, I was sent by Jane to a Parisian school for foreign female students, 'Mademoiselle Anita's', run by Catholic nuns, where the pupils were not allowed to go in or out of the building without wearing gloves. A lot of the students in this dreary place spoke no French at all.

The lodgings Jane had found for me were in Passy (a staid, respectable arrondissement of Paris where I never felt comfortable), in a dark apartment belonging to two widows of military men who — prior to the Americans' involvement in Vietnam — had fought and died in Indo-China.

Both the school and the flat (where my breakfast was weak coffee served with pieces of antique baguette, often containing weevils) made me so miserable that I at last discovered in myself the deep anger with my mother that I should have found at Crofton Grange. And this, in the Gauloises-scented, jazz-inflected air of Paris in 1961, propelled me into all-out rebellion. I unilaterally discharged myself from Mademoiselle Anita's school and, helped by a friend I'd met in Switzerland, Miranda Reid, enrolled myself at the Sorbonne, on the Cours de Civilisation, built around French literature, history and philosophy. Here, at last (in the days

when you could eat steak and chips on the Boul'
Mich for six francs), I began to lead a liberating
student life.

Jane was, of course, furious when I came home
at Christmas and told her what I'd done, but
perhaps she saw that, at eighteen — in ever more
Juliette Gréco mode of dress and make-up — I'd
finally found the will to stand up to her wrong
decisions. I'd also got myself away from Passy
and into the flat where Miranda lodged with a
kindly, bohemian woman called Madame Dennis,
in the rue de Grenelle, off Saint-Germain-des-
Prés, where boyfriends were allowed to visit.

These arrangements were presented to Jane as
a fait accompli, and she was forced to go along
with them or keep me grounded at home, and
she didn't want that, thank you very much. Thus,
the remainder of my year in the great City of
Light was filled with wild endeavour. As well as
studying and devouring museums and galleries, I
went go-karting, gliding, dancing at jazz clubs
and swimming in the Seine. And I once again
began writing.

I was still Rosie. I couldn't rid myself of that
hated name until I finally went to university
(UEA, in Norwich, always referred to by Jane as
'that ropey university') in 1964. But in Paris,
Rosie had at last become more stubborn and
bold. Like Mary Ward in *Sacred Country*, she'd
understood that the wearing of a 'thistledown'
dress need not always suggest lightness and
decorum. It can be sabotaged and mocked if the
wearer dares to come vaulting onto the stage in
her wellington boots.

That stage at last began to light up for me in 1976, the year I published my first novel, *Sadler's Birthday*, at the age of thirty-three. It was rejected by six publishers, but finally landed on the desk of Penelope Hoare, then at Macdonald & Jane's, who took a risk on it. She was my editor and friend — through the publication of more than twenty books (with Hamish Hamilton, Sinclair-Stevenson and Chatto & Windus) — until her death in 2017.

Thanks to Penny, and to a gift I discovered in myself for perseverance, it became possible for me to put together a writing life as I'd imagined it from early childhood onwards. But it took me seventeen years after eating my last marshmallow with Robbie to begin to realise the hopes I'd shared with her under my mural of Milton's *L'Allegro* and *Il Penseroso* on the English room wall. This was a longer time than I had been alive as 'Rosie'.

# List of Illustrations

NOTE: All photos are property of the author

**First plate section**

Jane Thomson, Rose's mother, age 20, 1933
Keith Thomson, Rose's father, age 35, 1947
Linkenholt Manor, home of Roland and Mabel
 Dudley, Rose's grandparents, c. 1950
Rose's first birthday picnic, 2 August 1944
David's Cottage, where Rose saw the birds on
 the wire
Michael Dudley, Rose's uncle, ready for war, 1940
Nan and Jane outside 22 Sloane Avenue, 1950
Rose and Jo in Wengen with Nan, 1950
Rose near the Meadows canal with Piggy, Mary
 and Polly, 1954
Timmy Trusted with family Pekinese in Cornwall,
 c. 1950
Jane with Jo and the cousins, Jonathan and
 Robert, Swanage, 1951
School photo, Crofton Grange, 1953
Painting scenery for *The Mysteries of Udolpho*:
 with Jane McKenzie, Elsa Buckley and Rose
Rose's last school report, defaced by V.M.T.

**Second plate section**

Signed photo of Poet Laureate John Masefield in
 his Oxford study, 1959

Frilsham Manor in the 1960s
The 'ginnery' at Frilsham
Rose being 'finished' at Les Diablerets, Switzerland, 1960
On the balcony at Chardon: with Ginny Lathbury, Rose and Carol Reunert
Fondue at the Cafe de la Poste, Les Diablerets; with Rose, Jenny Lowe, Pierrette Monod and Carol Reunert
Ski instructor Monsieur Borloz — 'tits to the valley'
Happy at last?: Ivo and Jane Thomson fishing in Ireland, c. 1980
Loving Eleanor: Jane with Rose and baby Eleanor, 1972
Trying to love Mother: Rose with Jane, 1992
Smokers' corner: Richard Holmes with Jane at High House, Norfolk, 1993
Rose with Mawkie at the Lychgate, Linkenholt, 2002